PENGUIN CLASSICS

SIX RECORDS OF A FLOATING LIFE

ADVISORY EDITOR: BETTY RADICE

LEONARD PRATT began his Chinese studies as an undergraduate at the University of Michigan, and continued them in the graduate and fellowship programmes at Columbia University. He furthered his Chinese language studies in Taiwan from 1969 to 1974, and he is now the bureau chief for NBC News in Hong Kong.

CHIANG SU-HUI was born and educated in Taiwan. She has a degree in Chinese law, and has worked as an educator, writer and broadcaster.

Shen Fu

Six Records of a Floating Life

Translated with an Introduction and Notes by
Leonard Pratt and Chiang Su~hui

Penguin Books

PENGUIN BOOKS

Published by the Penguin Group
Penguin Books Ltd, 80 Strand, London WC2R 0RL, England
Penguin Putnam Inc., 375 Hudson Street, New York, New York 10014, USA
Penguin Books Australia Ltd, 250 Camberwell Road, Camberwell, Victoria 3124, Australia
Penguin Books Canada Ltd, 10 Alcorn Avenue, Toronto, Ontario, Canada M4V 3B2
Penguin Books India (P) Ltd, 11 Community Centre, Panchsheel Park, New Delhi – 110 017, India
Penguin Books (NZ) Ltd, Cnr Rosedale and Airborne Roads, Albany, Auckland, New Zealand
Penguin Books (South Africa) (Pty) Ltd, 24 Sturdee Avenue, Rosebank 2196, South Africa

Penguin Books Ltd, Registered Offices: 80 Strand, London WC2R 0RL, England

www.penguin.com

This translation first published 1983
27

Printed in England by Clays Ltd, St Ives plc
Filmset in Monophoto Sabon

Maps on pages 166–7 by Reginald Piggott

ISBN-13: 978–0–140–44429–2

Contents

Now the heavens and earth are the hostels of creation; and time has seen a full hundred generations. Ah, this floating life, like a dream . . . True happiness is so rare!

LI PO, 'On a Banquet with my Cousins on a Spring Night in the Peach Garden'

Introduction

Shen Fu was born in Soochow in the latter part of the eighteenth century, at the height of the Ch'ing Dynasty. He was a government clerk, a painter, occasional trader, and a tragic lover, and in his mid forties he set out his life in six moving 'records' that have delighted the Chinese ever since they came to light in the nineteenth century.

While it is much more, the *Six Records* is known among the Chinese as a love story. As such, from a Western point of view, it is unique. For though it is indeed a true love story of Shen Fu and his wife Yün, it is a love story set in a traditional Chinese society – and thus their love coexists and intermingles with Shen Fu's affairs with courtesans, and with his wife's attempts to find him a concubine. And yet, for all that, it is none the less love.

The role of the courtesan as described in the *Six Records* is an example of what makes the book a valuable social document. It is difficult for Westerners to understand just what a courtesan in China was, because the only equivalent we have for the role is a prostitute. But a courtesan properly called was respectable and respected, and her sexual favours were by no means necessarily for sale. As van Gulik has described in his classic *Sexual Life in Ancient China* (Humanities Press, Atlantic Highlands, N.J., 1974), a courtesan could often be more independent and powerful than the men she ostensibly served. It is this kind of small but significant alteration to our perceptions and presumptions which the *Six Records* can effect that makes it so important a book for Westerners.

Chinese readers find something else in it. It must be recalled how common arranged marriages were among the Chinese until quite recently. Even now, a great deal of parental influence, or economic or social coercion, is still present as an influence in the choice of marriage partners in many Chinese societies.

And so a book arising out of the Imperial literary tradition that extolled enduring, romantic love easily became, and has remained, a favourite among Chinese readers: it has recently been reissued in China by the People's Literature Publishing Society, and is certainly the first primarily romantic book to come out in China for decades.

Shen Fu has described his life with his wife in what is probably the most frank and moving story to come to us from the literature of his time. He has given us a remarkable picture of Yün, his child love and his wife. Her life was hard but she played on all its graces, and Shen Fu's portrait of her manages to infuse the greatest tenderness into what is one of the most realistic accounts of the life of a woman ever given in traditional Chinese literature.

The book's remarkable frankness is broader than that, however. Official literature of the Imperial period, of course, tells us little of the daily life of the more ordinary Chinese people. Novels, plays, and tales of mystery do tell us a bit, but are often so taken up with details of their plots that there is little space left over to tell how people living in China then actually spent their time. The *Six Records* does tell us in great detail, while managing to avoid many of what must seem to Western readers to be the convolutions that plague so much Chinese popular literature of the time. Fortunately for us, Shen Fu accomplished a rare feat in traditional China: he became literate without becoming a *literatus*.

Shen Fu was, by his standards and by our own, a conspicuous failure in many ways. The highest he rose officially was to the position of private secretary to a powerful friend, a role that fell to many luckless *literati* of the Ch'ing. He was not much of a painter, he was a poor businessman frequently in debt, and by the end of his book he seems to have become entirely estranged from his family.

Yet while he was so often a victim, he was still determinedly upright when the chance to be so came his way. He resigned one official post in disgust at his colleagues' misdeeds, and he is gentleman enough not to tell us what they did that so upset him. He restored a peasant girl to her family when a man of influence was trying to force her to become a concubine. He was a trusting friend, often to his cost.

If Shen Fu was a failure in so many ways, much of his failure was related to the class from which he came – the *yamen* private secretary. The secretaries in a *yamen* – a government office – were failures almost by definition.

The origin of the profession of *yamen* secretary lay in two uniquely Chinese administrative practices. The first was a rule against assigning magistrates to their home districts. Throughout the post-feudal Chinese dynasties this was a standard means of attempting to ensure that officials administered their districts honestly, unswayed by local loyalties or favourites.

The second practice arose from the Chinese determination that government officials should be scholars first and bureaucrats second. One of the largest empires in the history of the world was administered by a small group of men who, prior to their first assignment, had not had the slightest training in administration, and who knew more about the poetry of a thousand years before than they did about tax law.

The typical Chinese magistrate, therefore, found himself in a district of which he had little personal knowledge – indeed, he might be woefully ignorant even of the local dialect of the language – and with only the slightest acquaintance with the complex laws and customs by which he was supposed to carry out his manifold responsibilities. He needed help, and he found it in the private secretary.

Literate and technically skilled, the private secretary was the magistrate's link between the scholarly ethics and the practical realities of Imperial Chinese government. T'ung-tsu Ch'ü (*Local Government in China Under the Ch'ing*, Harvard University Press, 1962) divides the secretaries into seven categories of specialists: law, tax administration, tax collection, registration of documents, correspondence, preparation of documents, and book-keeping. It is nowhere stated clearly in the *Six Records*, but Shen Fu seems to have specialized in law, the most prestigious of the seven.

The secretaries prepared almost every document a magistrate saw. They recommended decisions for him, handled virtually all his official correspondence, helped organize court sessions, and drafted replies on his behalf to official queries about his actions, actions which probably had been recommended by themselves in the first place. The quality of his secretaries could make or break a magistrate's career; they were very powerful.

They were also very unofficial. Except for one brief and unsuccessful experiment, the Ch'ing Dynasty never officially recognized their existence. They were the employees of the magistrate – not of the government – recruited by him and paid out of his personal funds. They were well paid – Ch'ü estimates they were the only members of a *yamen* staff able to support themselves on their salaries – and well respected. Whenever Shen Fu records going to work for a magistrate, he describes himself as being 'invited' to take the position; this is not an affectation. Once employed, the secretaries were far more than servants; resignation in protest was far from uncommon and, as noted above, Shen Fu himself seems to have done it at least once.

Who were the private secretaries, and where did they come from? Since they were well educated – they had to be in order to do their jobs – most had, on one or more occasions, taken the examinations which were the natural culmination of the education system of the day. If they had passed those examinations – and some of course did – they would have become officials themselves, rather than secretaries. We are talking, therefore, about a group of men who had either denied, or had been denied, entrance to the scholar-official class; men who had studied for the highest posts and failed to attain even the lowest.

It must have been a painful situation. Raised in the traditions of China's greatest poets and administrators, they were forced to live the only life their world offered them – itinerant and temporary employees, their only domain the shadowy world of *yamen* clerks, their only power that derived from their patron, towards whom it would have been only natural to feel a certain amount of jealousy.

All this must be kept in mind in considering what sort of man Shen Fu was, for it must be admitted that on the surface there are a fair number of unpleasant things about him. Perhaps the most difficult to understand is his repeated failure to provide for his family, apparently because it might not fit in with his image of himself. When his wife was ill and needed medicine, for example, he opened a shop to sell paintings – which he admits brought in only enough money to buy part of the medicine she needed – rather (we must unkindly note) than taking on a lower-status job that might have given him a more than occasional income.

Such facts are quite unquestionable; Shen Fu himself sets them out, though not as harshly as we have just done. So how much of a scoundrel was he? We leave that for the ultimate judgement of the reader, but we do think there are several points that ought to be remembered in making that judgement.

True, Shen Fu was a terrible romantic, a dreamer, often a victim of self-deception. But it should be noted that the education he received was intended exclusively to fit him for a part in life as a scholar-administrator; and beyond that education, no one of his class had much training at all. True, Shen Fu seems to us to cling to that education long after it has become irrelevant to his life; but perhaps he simply believed its promises, or was more enraptured by its graces, than others would have been. On a more practical level, it is worth asking what other profession he would have been suited for, had he decided to try to find something else to do; or, for that matter, what other profession his all-powerful parents would have allowed him to take up.

While granting all his personal faults, it seems to us that Shen Fu's inability to assume responsibility was not really due to them. He was dealing with a difficult life with the only set of rules he understood; his tragedy was that they were not enough to see him through. It was this same tragedy that, a few decades after his book was written, began to overtake all his countrymen.

The original text of the book as we have it today is incomplete. The last two of the *Six Records* were lost before a manuscript of the book was discovered and published for the first time in the 1870s. During the 1930s the World Book Company published in Shanghai what it claimed was a complete text of the book discovered by one Wang Ch'ün-ch'ing in Soochow; in this form the book has recently gone through several impressions in Taiwan. The last two *Records* which it presents are known to be false, however, having been copied from works by other authors; details of these forgeries appear in two brief appendices to this translation. Apart from these pieces of information, we can add only the testimony of Shen Fu himself that he was working on the book in 1809.

The quality of the book presents some challenges. By his own admission, Shen Fu was not always the most explicit of writers. There are references in the book that are not clear, some that make little sense. Sometimes his facts are not consistent. There are also great differences between our modern ideas and Shen Fu's of just what a book ought to be. The *Six Records* is not the chronologically constructed tale that we are now used to reading. Instead, Shen Fu takes particular topics and follows them each through his life, one at a time; the book is thus intended to be six different layers that add up to a 'floating life', each layer having little regard for its relationship to any other. Where we expect transitions, Shen Fu gives us few, and where we expect logical explanations he often gives us none. Sentences frequently stand almost by themselves. The book is meant to be mused over and, by our standards, read very slowly. There is much that is left unsaid. What is said, however, is rich in the life of the times. The troubled black sheep of a declining family, Shen Fu has left us a lively portrait of his era that in places strikes chords which are remarkably resonant with those of our own times.

It would be unusual if such a work had not come to the attention of translators before. Lin Yutang first translated the book in 1935, when it was serialized in the *T'ien Hsia Monthly* and in *Hsi Feng*. His translation of the entire book has appeared in several editions.

With the greatest respect for our predecessor, however, we felt that there was room for a full translation of the *Six Records* into modern English which would – by the use of extensive but, we hope, not intrusive notes and maps – present to the modern English reader a more complete exposition of the tale Shen Fu told. He wrote for an audience of his own time and place, and neither of those will ever live again. We hope that our contribution to this work may help it to live in the minds of today's Western readers, as its author intended it should live in the minds of his contemporaries.

We have tried to provide a complete translation that is, in the words of Anthony C. Yu, 'the most intelligible fidelity to the original'. Corrections to our work are inevitable, and we welcome them with the respect which is due to the original.

Chronology

When Shen Fu wrote the *Six Records* he made little attempt to organize the story of his life chronologically. For readers who may find it helpful, the following is taken from information provided by the book itself.

1763 Shen Fu was born, ten months after his wife-to-be.

1775 He met Yün for the first time, and his mother arranged their marriage; they were thirteen years old. The affair of the rice porridge occurred in this year.

1778 He began his travels around Hangchou while studying there. He took some examinations during this time.

1780 Shen Fu and Yün were married at the age of seventeen.

1781 His father fell ill, and Shen Fu was introduced to the profession of *yamen* private secretary. In the winter of this year he met his friend, the short-lived Hung-kan.

1783 He accepted a position at Weiyang (Yangchou), apparently his first independent posting.

1786 Yün gave birth to their daughter, Ching-chün.

1788 Shen Fu left official life in disgust after an unspecified incident at Chihsi. He tried his hand at trade during this year, but failed. His son Feng-sen was born.

1790 While Shen Fu worked with his father at Hungchiang, Yün upset the family by mishandling arrangements to obtain a concubine for her father-in-law.

1792   This year they were expelled from the family after a mis-understanding which involved Yün with a loan that had not been repaid by Shen Fu's younger brother. They moved to the Villa of Serenity, where they lived for a year and a half. It was during this period that Shen Fu left on his profligate business trip to Canton.

1794   In the seventh month of this year Shen Fu returned from Canton. Shortly after his return, the matter of the loan was cleared up and they were allowed to return home.

1795   They met Han-yüan, the sing-song girl.

1800   Shen Fu paid his visit to the abandoned Wuyin Temple. Later in the year he and Yün were again expelled from the family, after he once more got involved in a quarrel about a loan, and after the family had become upset over Yün's continuing friendship with Han-yüan. At the end of the year they moved to stay with friends, the Huas at Hsishan, and Yün saw their children, then aged twelve and fourteen, for the last time.

1801   A year of borrowing from Shen Fu's brother-in-law and a friend. For most of this year and the next Shen Fu worked at the Hanchiang (Yangchou) Salt Bureau, while Yün remained at Hsishan.

1802   Yün's health improved and she moved to join her husband at Yangchou. Shortly after that, he lost his job.

1803   Yün sickened again and died at Yangchou in the spring at the age of forty.

1804   Shen Fu's father died. Late in the year Shen Fu visited the Yungtai Sands with his share-cropping friend Hsia Yi-shan.

1805   In the first month of this year he visited the Sea of Fragrant Flowers on Pu Mountain with Hsia Yi-shan. In September he became a retainer of his childhood friend Shih Cho-tang and began a journey with him to take up office in Szechuan.

1806   The party wintered at Chingchon in Hupei Province, then went on to Shantung in the tenth month. Shen Fu heard by letter that his son Feng-sen had died.

1807   Shen Fu moved to Peking in the autumn, when his patron Shih Cho-tang was assigned to the Hanlin Academy. While the text of the *Six Records* does not contain the information, it is known that Shen Fu in this year was appointed secretary to a diplomatic mission sent from the court in Peking to give Chinese recognition to a new king of the Ryukyu Islands.

1809   During the year Shen Fu was writing the *Six Records*, at the age of forty-six. Nothing is known of his life after this.

Weights and Measures

It was only after their revolutions that the Chinese truly began to unify their weights and measures. Standardization had begun in the mid nineteenth century with so-called 'treaty port' measures, but these were adopted largely for purposes of foreign trade and had little relevance to the rest of the country, where a complex and often contradictory system of local customs and usages continued to apply. Shen Fu was writing some decades before even the treaty port measures were introduced, moreover, so we would be misleading the reader if we offered the following as anything more than an approximate guide.

The catty   A catty is customarily a measure of weight, 'standardized' in the nineteenth century at 1⅓ lbs. Shen Fu uses it as a capacity measure for wine, however, and as such it is usually taken to be equal to a pint.

The *chang*   One *chang* is equal to 10 Chinese feet. In treaties of the nineteenth century the Chinese foot was defined as 14 English inches, which would make a *chang* equal to 11 feet 8 inches.

The *jen*   An archaic measure equal to 7 Chinese feet, and thus to 8 English feet by treaty port definition.

The *li*   The length of the *li*, or Chinese mile, has varied greatly with time, place, and circumstance. It is customarily taken to be about ⅓ of an English mile. Frequently, however, the *li* was less a measure of distance than it was a measure of effort required to cover a given distance; an uphill road would measure more *li* on the ascent than it would on the descent.

The *mou*   The Chinese acre, which is usually converted at the rate set by nineteenth-century treaty in Shanghai as being equal to $\frac{1}{6}$ of an English acre. By local practice, however, it could vary anywhere from $\frac{1}{15}$ to $\frac{1}{3}$ of an English acre. There are some indications that this variation may be accounted for by varying productivity of the land at the time the local standard was set. The real definition of a *mou* would thus be the amount of land required to produce a given yield, and a *mou* of high-quality land would be smaller than a *mou* of low-quality land. Local variations make this very difficult to establish with certainty, however.

The stone   The picul, which could be either a capacity or a weight measure. Given the Chinese preference for weight measures it seems to us that this is what is intended here, and as such it was standardized at 133 lbs. Its real meaning varied greatly from place to place, however.

Translators' Note

All romanization of Chinese names follows the Wade-Giles system; however, out of consideration for the general reader we have omitted aspiration marks in the body of the text, while retaining them in the notes. We have given Chinese place-names in English only where we believed they would make some sense in translation.

PART I

The Joys of the Wedding Chamber

I was born in the winter of the 27th year of the reign of the Emperor Chien Lung,[1] on the second and twentieth day of the eleventh month. Heaven blessed me, and life then could not have been more full. It was a time of great peace and plenty, and my family was an official one that lived next to the Pavilion of the Waves[2] in Soochow. As the poet Su Tung-po wrote, 'All things are like spring dreams, passing with no trace.' If I did not make a record of that time, I should be ungrateful for the blessings of heaven.

The very first of the three hundred chapters of the *Book of Odes* concerns husbands and wives, so I too will write of other matters in their turn. Unfortunately I never completed my studies, so my writing is not very skilful. But here my purpose is merely to record true feelings and actual events. Criticism of my writing will be like the shining of a bright light into a dirty mirror.

When I was young I was engaged to Chin Sha-yu, but she died when she was eight years old. Eventually I married Chen Yün, the daughter of my uncle, Mr Chen Hsin-yü. Her literary name was Shu-chen.[3]

Even while small, she was very clever. While she was learning to talk she was taught the poem *The Mandolin Song*[4] and could repeat it almost immediately.

Yün's father died when she was four years old, leaving her mother, whose family name was Chin, and her younger brother, Ko-chang. At first they had virtually nothing, but as Yün grew older she became very adept at needlework, and the labour of her ten fingers came to provide for all three of them. Thanks to her work, they were always able to afford to pay the tuition for her brother's teachers.

One day Yün found a copy of *The Mandolin Song* in her

brother's book-box and, remembering her lessons as a child, was able to pick out the characters one by one. That is how she began learning to read. In her spare moments she gradually learned how to write poetry, one line of which was, 'We grow thin in the shadows of autumn, but chrysanthemums grow fat with the dew.'

When I was thirteen, my mother took me along on a visit to her relatives. That was the first time I met my cousin Yün, and we two children got on well together. I had a chance to see her poems that day, and though I sighed at her brilliance I privately feared she was too sensitive to be completely happy in life. Still, I could not forget her, and I remember saying to my mother, 'If you are going to choose a wife for me, I will marry no other than Yün.'

Mother also loved her gentleness, so she was quick to arrange our engagement, sealing the match by giving Yün a gold ring from her own finger. This was in the 39th year of the reign of the Emperor Chien Lung,[5] on the 16th day of the seventh month.

That winter mother took me to their home once again, for the marriage of Yün's cousin. Yün and I were born in the same year, but because she was ten months older than I, I had always called her 'elder sister', while she called me 'younger brother'. We continued to call one another by these names even after we were engaged.

At her cousin's wedding the room was full of beautifully dressed people. Yün alone wore a plain dress; only her shoes were new. I noticed they were skilfully embroidered, and when she told me she had done them herself I began to appreciate that her cleverness lay not only in her writing.

Yün had delicate shoulders and a stately neck, and her figure was slim. Her brows arched over beautiful, lively eyes. Her only blemish was two slightly protruding front teeth, the sign of a lack of good fortune. But her manner was altogether charming, and she captivated all who saw her.

I asked to see more of her poems that day, and found some had only one line, others three or four, and most were unfinished. I asked her why.

'I have done them without a teacher,' she replied, laughing. 'I hope you, my best friend, can be my teacher now and help me finish them.' Then as a joke I wrote on her book, 'The Embroidered Bag of Beautiful Verses'. I did not then realize that the origin of her early death already lay in that book.

That night after the wedding I escorted my relatives out of the city, and it was midnight by the time I returned. I was terribly hungry and asked for something to eat. A servant brought me some dried plums, but they were too sweet for me. So Yün secretly took me to her room, where she had hidden some warm rice porridge and some small dishes of food. I delightedly picked up my chopsticks, but suddenly heard Yün's cousin Yu-heng call, 'Yün, come quickly!'

Yün hurriedly shut the door and called back, 'I'm very tired. I was just going to sleep.' But Yu-heng pushed open the door and came in anyway.

He saw me just about to begin eating the rice porridge, and chuckled, looking out of the corner of his eye at Yün. 'When I asked you for some rice porridge just now, you said there wasn't any more! But I see you were just hiding it in here and saving it for your "husband"!'

Yün was terribly embarrassed, and ran out. The whole household broke into laughter. I was also embarrassed and angry, roused my servant, and left early.

Every time I returned after that, Yün would hide. I knew she was afraid that everyone would laugh at her.

On the night of the 22nd day of the first month in the 44th year of the reign of the Emperor Chien Lung[6] I saw by the light of our wedding candles that Yün's figure was as slim as before. When her veil was lifted we smiled at each other. After we had shared the ceremonial cup of wine and sat down together for the wedding banquet, I secretly took her small hand under the table. It was warm and it was soft, and my heart beat uncontrollably.

I asked her to begin eating, but it turned out to be a day on which she did not eat meat, a Buddhist practice which she had followed for several years. I thought to myself that she had begun this practice at the very time I had begun to break out with acne, and I asked her, 'Since my skin is now clear and healthy, couldn't you give up this custom?' Her eyes smiled amusement, and her head nodded agreement.

That same night of the 22nd there was a wedding-eve party for my elder sister. She was to be married on the 24th, but the 23rd was a day of national mourning[7] on which all entertaining was forbidden and the holding of the wedding-eve party would have been impossible. Yün attended the dinner, but I spent the time in our bedroom drinking with my sister's maid of honour. We played a drinking game which I lost frequently, and I wound up getting very drunk and falling asleep. By the time I woke up the next morning, Yün was already putting on her make-up.

During the day a constant stream of relatives and friends came to congratulate Yün and me on our marriage. In the evening there were some musical performances in honour of the wedding, after the lamps had been lit.

At midnight I escorted my sister to her new husband's home, and it was almost three in the morning when I returned. The candles had burned low and the house was silent. I stole quietly into our room to find my wife's servant dozing beside the bed and Yün herself with her make-up off but not yet asleep. A candle burned brightly beside her; she was bent intently over a book, but I could not tell what it was that she was reading with such concentration. I went up to her, rubbed her shoulder, and said, 'You've been so busy these past few days, why are you reading so late?'

Yün turned and stood up. 'I was just thinking of going to sleep, but I opened the bookcase and found this book, *The Romance of the Western Chamber*.[8] Once I had started reading it, I forgot how tired I was. I had often heard it spoken of, but this was the first time I had had a chance to read it. The author really is as talented as people say, but I do think his tale is too explicitly told.'

I laughed and said, 'Only a talented writer could be so explicit.'

Yün's servant then urged us to go to sleep, but we told her she should go to sleep first, and to shut the door to our room. We sat up making jokes, like two close friends meeting after a long separation. I playfully felt her breast and found her heart was beating as fast as mine. I pulled her to me and whispered in her ear, 'Why is your heart beating so fast?' She answered with a bewitching smile that made me feel a love so endless it shook my soul. I held her close as I parted the curtains and led her into bed. We never noticed what time the sun rose in the morning.

As a new bride, Yün was very quiet. She never got angry, and when anyone spoke to her she always replied with a smile. She was respectful to her elders and amiable to everyone else. Everything she did was orderly, and was done properly. Each morning when she saw the first rays of the sun touch the top of the window, she would dress quickly and hurry out of bed, as if someone were calling her. I once laughed at her about it; 'This is not like that time with the rice porridge! Why are you still afraid of someone laughing at you?'

'True,' she answered, 'my hiding the rice porridge for you that time has become a joke. But I'm not worried about people laughing at me now. I am afraid your parents will think I'm lazy.'

While I would have liked it if she could have slept more, I had to agree that she was right. So every morning I got up early with her, and from that time on we were inseparable, like a man and his shadow. Words could not describe our love.

We were so happy that our first month together passed in the twinkling of an eye. At that time my father, the Honourable Chia-fu, was working as a private secretary in the prefectural government office at Kuichi.[9] He sent for me, having enrolled me as a student of Mr Chao Sheng-chai at Wulin.[10] Mr Chao taught me patiently and well; the fact that I can write at all today is due to his efforts.

I had, however, originally planned to continue my studies with my father after my marriage, so I was disappointed when I received his letter. I feared Yün would weep when she heard of it, but she showed no emotion, encouraged me to go, and helped me pack my bag. The night before I left she was slightly subdued, but that was all. When it was time for me to go, though, she whispered to me, 'There will be no one there to look after you. Please take good care of yourself.'

My boat cast off just as the peach and the plum flowers were in magnificent bloom. I felt like a bird that had lost its flock. My world was shaken. After I arrived at the offices where my father worked, he immediately began preparations to go east across the river.

Our separation of three months seemed as if it were ten years long. Yün wrote to me frequently, but her letters asked about me twice as often as they told me anything about herself. Most of what she wrote was merely to encourage me in my studies, and the rest was just polite chatter. I really was a little angry with her. Every time the wind would rustle the bamboo trees in the yard, or the moon would shine through the leaves of the banana tree outside my window, I would look out and miss her so terribly that dreams of her took possession of my soul.

My teacher understood how I felt, and wrote to tell my father about it. He then assigned me ten compositions and sent me home for a while to write them. I felt like a prisoner who has been pardoned.

Once I was on the boat each quarter of an hour seemed to pass as slowly as a year. After I got home and paid my respects to my mother, I went into our room and Yün rose to greet me. She held my hands without saying a word. Our souls became smoke and mist. I thought I heard something, but it was as if my body had ceased to exist.

It was then the sixth month, and steamy hot in our room. Fortunately we lived just west of the Pavilion of the Waves' Lotus Lovers' Hall, where it was cooler. By a bridge and overlooking a stream there was a small hall called My Desire, because, as desired, one could 'wash my hat strings in it when it is clean, and wash my feet in it when it is dirty'.[11] Almost under the eaves of the hall there was an old tree that cast a shadow across the windows so deep that it turned one's face green. Strollers were always walking along the opposite bank of the stream. This was where my father, the Honourable Chia-fu, used to entertain guests privately, and I obtained my mother's permission to take Yün there to escape the summer's heat. Because it was so hot, Yün had given up her embroidery. She spent all day with me as I studied, and we talked of ancient times, analysed the moon, and discussed the flowers. Yün could not take much drink, and would accept at the most three cups of wine when I forced her to. I taught her a literary game, in which the loser has to drink a cup. We were certain two people had never been happier than we were.

One day Yün asked me, 'Of all the ancient literary masters, who do you think is the best?'

'*The Annals of the Warring States* and *Chuang Tsu* are known for their liveliness,' I replied. 'Kuang Heng and Liu Hsiang are known for their elegance. Shih Chien and Pan Ku are known for their breadth. Chang Li is known for his extensive knowledge, and Liu Chou for his vigorous style. Lu Ling is known for his originality, and Su Hsün and his two sons for their essays. There are also the policy debates of Chia and Tung, the poetic styles of Yü and Hsü, and the Imperial memorials of Lu Chih.[12] I could never give a complete list of all the talented writers there have been. Besides, which one you like depends upon which one you feel in sympathy with.'

'It takes great knowledge and a heroic spirit to appreciate ancient literature,' said Yün. 'I fear a woman's learning is not enough to master it. The only way we have of understanding it is through poetry, and I understand but a bit of that.'

'During the Tang Dynasty all candidates had to pass an examination in poetry before they could become officials,' I remarked. 'Clearly the best were Li Pai and Tu Fu.[13] Which of them do you like best?'

Yün said her opinion was that 'Tu Fu's poetry is very pure and carefully tempered, while Li Pai's is ethereal and open. Personally, I would rather have Li Pai's liveliness than Tu Fu's strictness.'

'But Tu Fu was the more successful, and most scholars prefer him. Why do you alone like Li Pai?'

'Tu Fu is alone,' Yün replied, 'in the detail of his verse and the vividness of his expression. But Li Pai's poetry flows like a flower tossed into a stream. It's enchanting. I would not say Li Pai is a better poet than Tu Fu, but only that he appeals to me more.'

I smiled and said, 'I never thought you were such an admirer of Li Pai's.'

Yün smiled back. 'Apart from him, there is only my first teacher, Mr Pai Lo-tien.[14] I have always had a feeling in my heart for him that has never changed.'

'Why do you say that?' I asked.

'Didn't he write *The Mandolin Song?*'

I laughed. 'Isn't that strange! You are an admirer of Li Pai's, and Pai Lo-tien was your first tutor. And as it happens, the literary name of your husband is San-pai. What is this affinity you have for the character *pai*?'[15]

Yün laughed and said, 'Since I do have an affinity for the character *pai*, I'm afraid that in the future my writing will be full of *pai* characters.' (Our Kiangsu accent pronounces the character *pieh* as *pai*.)[16] We both shook with laughter.

'Since you know poetry,' I said, 'you must know the good and bad points of the form called *fu*.'[17]

'I know it's descended from the ancient Chu Tzu poetry,'[18] Yün replied, 'but I have only studied it a little and it's hard to understand. Of the *fu* poets of the Han and Chin Dynasties, who had the best meter and the most refined language, I think Hsiang-ju was the best.'

I jokingly said, 'So perhaps Wen-chün did not fall in love with Hsiang-ju[19] because of the way he played the lute after all, but because of his poetry?' The conversation ended with us both laughing loudly.

I am by nature candid and unconstrained, but Yün was scrupulous and meticulously polite. When I would occasionally put a cape over her shoulders or help her adjust her sleeves, she would invariably say, 'I beg your pardon.' If I gave her a handkerchief or a fan, she would always stand to take it. At first I did not like her acting like this, and once I said to her, 'Do you think that by being so polite you can make me do as you like? For it is said that "Deceit hides behind too much courtesy".'

Yün blushed. 'Why should respect and good manners be called deceit?'

'True respect comes from the heart, not from empty words,' I said.

'There is no one closer to us than our parents,' Yün said, arguing with me now. 'But how could we merely respect them in our hearts while being rude in our treatment of them?'

'But I was only joking,' I protested.

'Most arguments people have begin with a joke,' Yün said. 'Don't ever argue with me for the fun of it again – it makes me so angry I could die!'

I pulled her close to me, patted her back, and comforted her. Her anger passed and she began to smile. From then on, the polite phrases 'How dare I?' and 'I beg your pardon' became mere expressions to us. We lived together with the greatest mutual respect for three and twenty years, and as the years passed we grew ever closer.

Whenever we would meet one another in a darkened room or a narrow hallway of the house, we would hold hands and ask, 'Where are you going?' We felt furtive, as if we were afraid others would see us. In fact, at first we even avoided being seen walking or sitting together, though after a while we thought nothing of it. If Yün were sitting and talking with someone and saw me come in, she would stand up and move over to me and I would sit down beside her. Neither of us thought about this and it seemed quite natural; and though at first we felt embarrassed about it, we gradually grew accustomed to doing it. The strangest thing to me then was how old couples seemed to treat one another like enemies. I did not understand why. Yet people said, 'Otherwise, how could they grow old together?' Could this be true? I wondered.

On the evening of the 7th day of the seventh month that year, Yün lit candles and set out fruit on the altar by the Pavilion of My Desire, and we worshipped Tien Sun[20] together. I had had two matching seals engraved with the inscription, 'May we remain husband and wife in all our lives to come'; on mine the characters were raised and on hers they were incised. We used them to sign the letters we wrote one another. That night the moonlight was very lovely, and as it was reflected in the stream it turned the ripples of the water as white as silk. We sat together near the water wearing light robes and fanned ourselves gently as we looked up at the clouds flying across the sky and changing into ten thousand shapes.

Yün said, 'The world is so vast, but still everyone looks up at the same moon. I wonder if there is another couple in the world as much in love as we are.'

'Naturally there are people everywhere who like to enjoy the night air and gaze at the moon,' I said, 'and there are more than a few women who enjoy discussing the sunset. But when a man and wife look at it together, I don't think it is the sunset they will wind up talking about.' The candles soon burned out, and the moon set. We took the fruit inside and went to bed.

The 15th day of the seventh month, when the moon is full, is the day called the Ghost Festival. Yün had prepared some small dishes, and we had planned to invite the moon to drink with us. But when night came, clouds suddenly darkened the sky.

Yün grew melancholy and said, 'If I am to grow old together with you, the moon must come out.'

I also felt depressed. On the opposite bank I could see will-o'-the-wisps winking on and off like ten thousand fireflies, as their light threaded through the high grass and willow trees that grew on the small island in the stream. To get ourselves into a better mood Yün and I began composing a poem out loud, with me offering the first couplet, her the second, and so on. After the first two couplets we gradually became less and less restrained and more and more excited, until we were saying anything that came into our heads. Yün was soon laughing so hard that she cried, and had to lean up against me, unable to speak a word. The heavy scent of jasmine in her hair assailed my nostrils, so to stop her laughing I patted her on the back and changed the subject, saying, 'I thought women of ancient times put jasmine flowers in their hair because they resembled pearls. I never realized that the jasmine is so attractive when mixed with the scent of women's make-up, much more attractive than the lime.'[21]

Yün stopped laughing. 'Lime is the gentleman of perfumes,' she said, 'and you notice its scent unconsciously. But the jasmine is a commoner that has to rely on a woman's make-up for its effect. It's suggestive, like a wicked smile.'

'So why are you avoiding the gentleman and taking up with the commoner?'

'I'm only making fun of gentlemen who love commoners,' she replied.[22]

Just as we were speaking, the water clock showed midnight. The wind gradually began to sweep the clouds away, and the full moon finally came out. We were delighted, and drank some wine leaning against the windowsill. But before we had finished three cups we heard a loud noise from under the bridge, as if someone had fallen into the water. We leaned out of the window and looked around carefully. The surface of the stream was as bright as a mirror, but we saw not a thing. We only heard the sound of a duck running quickly along the river bank. I knew that the ghosts of people who had drowned often appeared by the river near the Pavilion of the Waves, but I was worried that Yün would be afraid and so I did not dare tell her.

'Yi!' she said, none the less frightened for my silence. 'Where did that sound come from?'

We could not keep ourselves from trembling. I closed the window and we took the wine into the bedroom. The flame in the lamp was as small as a bean, and the curtains around the bed cast shadows that writhed like snakes. We were still frightened. I turned up the lamp and we got into bed, but Yün was already suffering hot and cold attacks from the shock. I caught the same fever, and we were ill for twenty days. It is true what people say, that happiness carried to an extreme turns into sadness. The events of that day were another omen that we were not to grow old together.

By the time of the Mid-Autumn Festival I had just started to feel better, though I was still a little weak. Yün had by this time been my wife for half a year without once going next door to the Pavilion of the Waves, so one evening I sent an old servant there to tell the gate-keeper not to let in any other visitors. Just as night was falling, Yün, my little sister, and I walked there. Two servants helped me along and another led the way. We crossed the stone bridge, went in at the gate, and took a small winding path along the eastern side of the gardens. There were rocks piled up into small artificial mountains, and trees with luxuriant light green leaves. The pavilion itself stood on top of a small hill. Steps led up to the summit, from where you could see all around for several miles. The smoke of cooking fires rose up from every direction into the brilliant twilight. On the opposite bank was a place called Chinshan Woods, where high officials would hold formal banquets; at that time the Chengyi Academy had not yet been established there. We had taken along a blanket which we spread out in the middle of the pavilion, and we all sat around in a circle on it, while the gate-keeper made tea and brought it up to us. A full moon soon rose above the trees, and we gradually felt a breeze beginning to tug at our sleeves. The moon shone on the stream below, and quickly drove away our cares.

'This is such fun!' said Yün. 'Wouldn't it be wonderful if we had a small skiff to row around in the stream down there?'

The time had come to light the lanterns, so, still thinking of the shock we had received on the night of the Ghost Festival, we left the pavilion and went home, holding hands all the way. It is a Soochow custom that on the night of the Mid-Autumn Festival women, regardless of whether they come from a well-off family or not, all come out in groups to stroll. This is called the 'moonlight walk'. But although the Pavilion of the Waves was elegant and peaceful, no one had come there that night.

My father, the Honourable Chia-fu, liked to adopt sons, so I had twenty-six brothers with surnames different from mine.[23] My mother too had adopted nine daughters; Miss Wang, the second of them, and Miss Yü, the sixth, got on best with Yün. Miss Wang was a simple girl who enjoyed drinking, while Miss Yü was open and loved to talk. Every time they got together they would exile me so that the three of them could sleep in the same bed. This was Miss Yü's idea.

'After you are married,' I once joked with her, 'I will invite your husband over and make him stay at least ten days.'

'I'll come along too,' she replied, 'and sleep with your wife. Won't that be fun?' Yün and Miss Wang said nothing, but only smiled.

At the time of my younger brother Chi-tang's marriage, we moved to Granary Lane, near the Drinking Horses Bridge. Although the new house was big, it was not as elegant as the one near the Pavilion of the Waves. For my mother's birthday that year we had an opera troupe come to perform, and Yün at first thought it was quite wonderful. My father had never been superstitious, however, so he had no compunctions about asking for the performance of *The Sad Parting*. The actors were excellent and, watching it, we were very moved.

But while the performance was still going on, I saw Yün suddenly get up from behind the screen where the women were seated and go to our room. After a long while she had still not returned, so I went in to look for her, Miss Yü and Miss Wang following me. We found Yün sitting alone beside the dressing table with her head in her hands.

'Are you unhappy about something?' I asked her.

'Seeing an opera is supposed to be entertaining,' Yün said. 'But today's is heartbreaking.'

Both Miss Yü and Miss Wang were laughing at her, but I told them they had to understand what a very emotional person she was. Still, Miss Yü asked her, 'Are you going to sit here by yourself all day?'

'When there's something I like, I'll go back and watch it,' Yün replied. Miss Wang went out as soon as she'd heard this, and asked my mother to tell them to perform things like *Tse Liang* and *Hou So*. After some urging Yün came out to watch, and soon began to cheer up.

My father's cousin, the Honourable Su-tsun, died young leaving no descendants, so my father named me to inherit from him.[24] His grave was on ancestral ground at Hsikuatang on the Mountain of Prosperity and Longevity, and every spring I had to take Yün there to sweep the grave and perform the rites. Second sister Wang had heard of a beautiful place on the mountain called the Ko Garden, and so she once asked to go along with us.

That day Yün saw some stones on the mountainside that were streaked with beautiful colours. 'If we put some in a bowl to make a little mountain,' she said, 'they would look even better than white stones from Hsüanchou.'

I told Yün I feared it would be hard to find enough stones to do that, but Miss Wang volunteered to collect them. She immediately went to the grave-keeper and borrowed a hempen bag, and then began collecting the stones, walking along as slowly and as deliberately as a crane. She would pick up each one, and if I said 'good' she would keep it; if I said 'no', she would throw it away.

Before long she was perspiring heavily and, dragging her bag, she came back to us and said, 'I don't have the strength to pick up any more.'

'I've heard that if you want to collect fruit in the mountains,' said Yün as she selected the stones she wanted, 'you have to get a monkey to do it for you. Now I know that that's true!'

Miss Wang rubbed her hands together furiously, as if she were going to tickle Yün in revenge for her joke. I stood between them to stop her, and scolded Yün. 'Miss Wang has been working while you've been relaxing, and still you talk like that. No wonder she's angry.'

On the way back we strolled through the Ko Garden, where the fresh, light green leaves and the delicate red flowers seemed to be competing over which was the most beautiful. Miss Wang always had been a foolish girl, and as soon as she saw the flowers she thought she had to pick some. Yün scolded her. 'You have no vase to put them in, and you're not going to put them in your hair either. Why are you picking so many?'

'They feel no pain,' Miss Wang said, 'so what's the harm?'

I laughed and told her, 'You are going to marry a pock-marked, hairy fellow. That will be the flowers' revenge.'

Miss Wang looked at me angrily, threw the flowers on the ground, and kicked them into a pond with her tiny foot. 'How can you make fun of me like this?' she said. But Yün joked with her, and her anger passed.

When we were first married Yün was very quiet, and enjoyed listening to me discuss things. But I drew her out, as a man will use a blade of grass to encourage a cricket to chirp, and she gradually became able to express herself, as the following conversation proves.

Every day Yün would mix her rice with tea. She liked to eat a spicy, salty kind of beancurd that Soochow people call 'stinking beancurd'. She also liked pickled cucumber. These last two were things I had hated all my life, so one day I said to her, 'Dogs have no stomach, and eat dung because they do not realize how bad it smells. A beetle rolls in its dung so it can become a cicada, because it wants to fly as high as it can. Which are you, a dog or a beetle?'

'That kind of beancurd is cheap,' Yün said, 'and it tastes good with either rice porridge or plain rice. I've eaten it since I was a child. As I am now living in your home I'm like the beetle that has become a cicada, and the reason I still like to eat the beancurd is that I have not forgotten my former life. As for pickled cucumber, the first time I had it was here in your home.'

'In other words, my house is a doghouse?' I said, continuing to joke with her.

Yün was embarrassed and quickly explained. 'There is dung in every house. The only question is whether one eats it.[25] I don't like garlic, but I still eat it because you like it. I would never ask you to eat stinking beancurd; but as for pickled cucumber, if you would only hold your nose and eat some you would realize how good it is. It's like the old stories about the girl named Wu-yen, who was ugly but virtuous.'[26]

'Now are you trying to get me to behave like a dog?'

'I've been acting like a dog for a long time,' Yün said. 'Why don't you try it?' Upon which she picked up a piece of pickled cucumber with her chopsticks and forced it into my mouth. I held my nose and chewed, and it did seem quite good. I took my hand away and continued chewing, and to my surprise found it did have rather a special taste. From then on, I too began to enjoy eating it.

Yün also ate salted beancurd by pouring sesame seed oil and a little sugar over it, and that was wonderful. She would sometimes eat the beancurd by mixing it with a paste of pickled cucumber; this she called 'double-delicious sauce', and it was very good.

One day I said to her, 'At first I did not like any of these things, but now I have come to like all of them very much. I cannot understand why.'

'If you like something,' said Yün, 'you don't care if it's ugly.'

My younger brother Chi-tang's wife is the granddaughter of Wang Hsü-chou. As the time for their marriage approached, she discovered she did not have enough pearl flowers.[27] Yün took out her own pearls that she had been given when we were married, and gave them to my mother for her to give to my brother's fiancée. The servants thought it was a pity that she should give up her own jewellery.

'Women are entirely *yin* in nature,' Yün told them, 'and pearls are the essence of *yin*. If you wear them in your hair, they completely overcome the spirit of *yang*. So why should I value them?'[28]

On the other hand, she prized shabby old books and tattered paintings. She would take the partial remnants of old books, separate them all into sections by topic, and then have them rebound. These she called her 'Fragments of Literature'. When she found some calligraphy or a painting that had been ruined, she felt she had to search for a piece of old paper on which to remount it. If there were portions missing, she would ask me to restore them. These she named the 'Collection of Discarded Delights'. Yün would work on these projects the whole day without becoming tired, whenever she could take time off from her sewing and cooking. If, in an old trunk or a shabby book, she came across a piece of paper with something on it, she acted as if she had found something very special. Every time our neighbour, old lady Fung, got hold of some scraps of old books, she would sell them to Yün.

Yün's habits and tastes were the same as mine. She understood what my eyes said, and the language of my brows. She did everything according to my expression, and everything she did was as I wished it.

Once I said to her, 'It's a pity that you are a woman and have to remain hidden away at home. If only you could become a man we could visit famous mountains and search out magnificent ruins. We could travel the whole world together. Wouldn't that be wonderful?'

'What is so difficult about that?' Yün replied. 'After my hair begins to turn white, although we could not go so far as to visit the Five Sacred Mountains, we could still visit places nearer by. We could probably go together to Hufu and Lingyen, and south to the West Lake and north to Ping Mountain.'[29]

'By the time your hair begins to turn white, I'm afraid you will find it hard to walk,' I told her.

'Then if we can't do it in this life, I hope we will do it in the next.'

'In our next life I hope you will be born a man,' I said. 'I will be a woman, and we can be together again.'

'That would be lovely,' said Yün, 'especially if we could still remember this life.'

I laughed. 'We still haven't finished talking about that business with the rice porridge when we were young. If in the next life we can still remember this one, we will have so much to talk about on our wedding night that we will never get to sleep!'

'People say that marriages are arranged by the "Old Man of the Moon",' said Yün. 'He has already pulled us together in this life, and in the next we will have to depend on him too. Why don't we have a picture of him painted so we can worship him?'

At that time the famous portraitist Chi Liu-ti, whose literary name was Chun, was living in Tiaohsi, and we asked him to paint the picture for us. He portrayed the old man carrying his red silk cord[30] in one hand, while with the other he grasped his walking stick with the *Book of Marriages* tied to the top of it. Though his hair was white, his face was that of a child, and he was striding through mist and fog. This was the best painting that Mr Chi ever did. My friend Shih Cho-tang wrote a complimentary inscription at the top of the painting, and I hung it in our room. On the 1st and the 15th days of each month, Yün and I would light incense and worship in front of it. Later, because of the many things that happened to our family, the painting was somehow lost and I have no idea in whose home it hangs now. 'Our next life is not known, while this life closes.' Our passion was so great. Will the Old Man understand and help us once again?

After we moved to Granary Lane, I called our upstairs bedroom the Pavilion of My Guest's Fragrance, after Yün's name[31] and the idea that husbands and wives should treat each other like guests. The new house had only a small garden and high walls, and there was nothing much that we liked about it. At the back there was a row of small rooms off the library, but when their windows were open there was nothing to see but the overgrown Lu Family Garden, which was a desolate sight. It was from this time that Yün began to miss the scenery of the Pavilion of the Waves.

There was then an old woman who lived east of the Chinmu Bridge and north of Keng Lane. Her cottage was surrounded by a vegetable garden, and had a rattan gate. Outside the gate there was a pond about one *mou* in size[32] that reflected the interwoven images of the flowers and the shadows of the trees. The place was the site of the ruins of the palace that Chang Shih-cheng had built at the end of the Yüan Dynasty.[33] Immediately to the west of her house there was a pile of broken bricks as big as a small hill, and if you climbed to the top you could see for a long way, a large area with few people and great wild beauty. The old woman once spoke of the place to Yün, who wanted very much to go and see it. 'Since we left the Pavilion of the Waves,' she told me, 'I dream about it night and day. As we cannot go back there, the only thing I can think of now is trying to find a substitute for it. What about this old woman's house?'

'In the worst heat of the early autumn,' I said, 'I think every morning of having a cool place to pass the long days. If you're interested, I'll have a look first and see whether the house is habitable. If it is, we could take our bedding and stay there for a month. What would you think of that?'

'I'm afraid your parents will disapprove,' Yün said.

I told her I would ask their permission myself, and the next day I went to look over the house. It had only two rooms, one in front and one at the back, each divided by a partition. The windows were paper and the bed of bamboo, and the place had altogether a subtle charm about it. When the old woman heard what we wanted, she was very happy to rent the bedroom to us. I pasted white paper up on the walls, and soon it looked like a different place entirely. I then respectfully informed my mother, and took Yün to live there.

Our only neighbours were an old couple who raised vegetables for a living. Learning we had come to escape the summer's heat, they came to call on us, bringing gifts of fish from the pond and vegetables from the garden. I tried to pay for them, but they would not take anything, so Yün made them some shoes, which we finally prevailed on them to accept.

It was then the beginning of the seventh month, with dark shadows among the green trees. There was a breeze across the water, and the songs of cicadas were everywhere. The old couple also made us a fishing pole, and I took Yün fishing in the deep shadows of the willow trees.

When the sun was going down, we would climb to the top of the small hill and admire the twilight. We used to make up impromptu poems there, one line of which was, 'Beast-like clouds eat the setting sun, the bow-like moon shoots falling stars.' After a while, when the moonlight fell directly into the pond and the sound of insects came from all around, we would move the bed out beside the fence. The old woman would come to tell us when the wine was warm and the food was hot. We would drink in the moonlight until we were a little tipsy, and then eat. After having a wash, we would fan ourselves with banana leaves, and sit or lie down and listen to our old neighbours telling stories of sin and retribution.[34] At three strokes of the night watch we would go in to sleep feeling cool and refreshed. It was almost like not living in the city at all.

We had asked the old couple to buy chrysanthemums and plant them all the way around the fence, and when the flowers bloomed in the ninth month I decided to stay there with Yün for ten more days. About then my mother came to visit us, and seemed quite happy with what she saw. We ate crabs beside the flowers, and thoroughly enjoyed the day.

'One day we should build a cottage here and buy ten *mou* of land to make a garden around it,' said Yün happily. 'We could have servants plant melons and vegetables that would be enough to live on. What with your painting and my embroidery, it would give us enough to have a little to drink while we wrote poetry. We could live quite happily wearing cotton clothes and eating nothing but vegetables and rice. We would never have to leave here.' I deeply wished we could do so. The cottage is still there, but now I have lost my most intimate friend. It is enough to make one sigh deeply.

About half a *li* from my house,[35] on Vinegar Warehouse Lane, was the Tungting Temple, which we usually called the Narcissus Temple.[36] Inside there were winding covered paths and a small park with pavilions. Every year on the god's birthday the members of each family association would gather in their corner of the temple, hang up a special glass lantern, and erect a throne below it. Beside the throne they would set out vases filled with flowers, in a competition to see whose decorations were most beautiful. During the day operas were performed, and at night candles of different lengths were set out among the vases and the flowers. This was called the 'lighting of the flowers'. The colours of the flowers, the shadows of the lamps, and the fragrant smoke floating up from the incense urns, made it all seem like a night banquet at the palace of the

Dragon King himself. The heads of the family associations would play the flute and sing, or brew fine tea and chat with one another. Townspeople gathered like ants to watch this spectacle, and a fence had to be put up under the eaves of the temple to keep them out.

One year some friends of mine invited me to go and help to arrange their flowers, so I had a chance to see the festival myself. I went home and told Yün how beautiful it was.

'What a shame that I cannot go just because I am not a man,' said Yün.

'If you wore one of my hats and some of my clothes, you could look like a man.'

Yün thereupon braided her hair into a plait and made up her eyebrows. She put on my hat, and though her hair showed a little around her ears it was easy to conceal. When she put on my robe we found it was an inch and a half too long, but she took it up around the waist and put on a riding jacket over it.

'What about my feet?' Yün asked.

'In the street they sell "butterfly shoes",' I said, 'in all sizes. They're easy to buy, and afterwards you can wear them around the house. Wouldn't they do?'

Yün was delighted, and when she had put on my clothes after dinner she practised for a long time, putting her hands into her sleeves and taking large steps like a man.

But suddenly she changed her mind. 'I am not going! It would be awful if someone found out. If your parents knew, they would never allow us to go.'

I still encouraged her to go, however. 'Everyone at the temple knows me. Even if they find out, they will only take it as a joke. Mother is at ninth sister's house, so if we come and go secretly no one will ever know.'

Yün looked at herself in the mirror and laughed endlessly. I pulled her along, and we left quietly. We walked all around inside the temple, with no one realizing she was a woman. If someone asked who she was, I would tell them she was my cousin. They would only fold their hands and bow to her.

At the last place we came to, young women and girls were sitting behind the throne that had been erected there. They were the family of a Mr Yang, one of the organizers of the festival. Without thinking, Yün walked over and began to chat with them as a woman quite naturally might, and as she bent over to do so she inadvertently laid her hand on the shoulder of one of the young ladies.

One of the maids angrily jumped up and shouted, 'What kind of a rogue are you, to behave like that!' I went over to try to explain, but Yün, seeing how embarrassing the situation could become, quickly took off her hat and kicked up her foot,[37] saying, 'See, I am a woman too!'

At first they all stared at Yün in surprise, but then their anger turned to laughter. We stayed to have some tea and refreshments with them, and then called sedan chairs and went home.

When Chien Shih-chu of Wuchiang County fell ill and died, my father wrote and ordered me to represent him at the funeral. Hearing this, Yün took me aside. 'If you are going to Wuchiang, you have to cross Lake Tai. I would love to go with you and see something more of the world.'

'I had just been thinking how lonely it would be going by myself,' I said, 'and that if you could come with me it would be lovely. But there is no excuse for you to go.'

'I could say I wanted to go home for a visit. You could go to the boat first, and I would meet you there.'

'Then on the way back we could stop the boat under Ten Thousand-Years Bridge,' I said. 'We could relax in the moonlight, the way we used to at the Pavilion of the Waves.'

It was then the 18th day of the sixth month. In the cool of the morning I took a servant and went ahead to the Hsü River Dock, where we boarded a boat and waited. Yün arrived in a sedan chair shortly afterwards. The boat cast off and left the Tiger's Roar Bridge, and after a while we began to see other sails in the wind, and birds on the sandy shore. The sky and the water became the same colour.

'Is this the Lake Tai that everyone speaks of?' asked Yün. 'Now that I see how grand the world is, I have not lived in vain! There are women who have lived their entire lives without seeing a vista like this.' It seemed we had only chatted for a little while before we arrived at Wuchiang, where the wind was rustling the willows along the bank.

I went ashore, only to return after the funeral to find the boat empty. I anxiously questioned the boatman, who pointed along the bank and said, 'Don't you see them in the shadow of the willows by the bridge watching the cormorants catch fish?'

To my surprise, Yün had gone ashore with the boatman's daughter. When I came up behind her she was still covered with perspiration, leaning against the other girl and lost in watching the birds.

I patted her shoulder and said, 'Your clothes are soaked through!'

Yün turned her head to look at me. 'I was afraid someone from the Chien family would come to the boat with you,' she said, 'so I came here for a while to keep them from seeing me if they did. Why did you come back so quickly?'

I laughed. 'So I could recapture you.'

We walked to the boat hand in hand, and sailed back to Ten Thousand-Years Bridge. The sun had not yet set by the time we reached the bridge, so we let down the windows of the boat to admit a breeze, then changed into silk clothes and, fanning ourselves, ate some melon to cool off. Before long the setting sun turned the bridge red, and the twilight mist enveloped the willows in darkness. The silver moon was just rising and the river quickly filled up with the lights of night fishermen. We sent our servant to the stern to drink with the boatman.

The boatman's daughter was named Su-yün, and she had had several cups of wine with me once before. She was quite nice, so I called her over and asked her to sit with Yün. There was no light in the bow of the boat, so we were able to enjoy the moon and drink happily. We began to play a literary drinking game, at which Su-yün could only blink her eyes.[38] She listened to us for quite a while, then said, 'I know a lot about drinking games, but I have never heard of this one. Will you teach it to me?'

Yün thought up several examples to try to explain it to her, but after some time the boat girl still did not understand.

I laughed and said, 'Stop it, lady teacher. I have a comparison that will explain the problem.'

'What kind of an example are you going to give?' Yün asked.

'A crane can dance but cannot plough, while an ox can plough but cannot dance. That is just the nature of things. Wouldn't it be a waste of time if you tried to teach each of them to play the other's game?'

Su-yün laughed playfully, hit me on the shoulder, and said, 'Are you making fun of me?'

At this Yün ordered us to stop. 'From now on we allow only talking. No more hitting! Whoever breaks the rule has to drink a big cup of wine.'

Su-yün had quite a capacity for wine, so she poured a big cup and downed it at one gulp.

'No hitting,' I then said, 'but surely it's all right if we caress one another.'

Yün laughed and pushed Su-yün over to me. 'Caress her to your heart's content, then.'

'Don't misunderstand me,' I said laughing. 'The whole point of caressing someone is to carry it off nonchalantly. Only a country boy would be rough about it.'

By this time the scent of jasmine in their hair had mixed with the aroma of the wine, all of it overlaid by the smell of perspiration in their make-up. It was quite overpowering.

'The stink of commoners fills the bow of this boat,' I joked. 'It's enough to make a man sick.'

At this Su-yün could not be stopped from hitting me repeatedly. 'Who told you to sniff around?' she shouted.

'You broke the rule,' Yün called out to her. 'I sentence you to two big cups!'

'But he called me a commoner. Why shouldn't I hit him?'

'He had a reason for using the word "commoner",' Yün told her. 'Drink these and I'll tell you.' So Su-yün drank the two big cups of wine one after the other, and Yün told her how we had joked about the jasmine one night when we lived at the Pavilion of the Waves.

'If that's what he was talking about,' Su-yün said, 'I should not

have blamed him. The sentence should be carried out once again.'
She then drank a third big cup of wine.

'I have heard what a beautiful voice you have,' Yün said as she
put the cup down. 'Could I hear one of your songs?'

Su-yün immediately began to sing, beating time on a small plate
with her ivory chopsticks. Yün was having so much fun she forgot
how much she was drinking. She became tipsy without even realizing it, so that she had to take a sedan chair and go home ahead of
me. I stayed a few moments longer for some tea and conversation
with Su-yün, and then walked home in the moonlight.[39]

At that time we were living with my friend Lu Pan-fang, at his
home, the Villa of Serenity. A few days after our trip Mrs Lu heard
some gossip, and took Yün aside. 'Yesterday I heard that your
husband had been seen drinking with two courtesans in a boat by
the Ten Thousand-Years Bridge. Did you know that?'

'It happened all right,' Yün replied, 'but one of those courtesans
was me.' Because she had brought it up, Yün then told her in detail
about our trip together. Hearing the explanation, Mrs Lu laughed
heartily and dropped the subject.

In the seventh month of the Chiayen year of the reign of the
Emperor Chien Lung[40] I returned from Yüehtung[41] with my friend
Hsü Hsiu-feng, who was my cousin's husband. He brought a new
concubine back with him, raving about her beauty to everyone, and
one day he invited Yün to go and see her. Afterwards Yün said to
Hsiu-feng, 'She certainly is beautiful, but she is not the least bit
charming.'

'If your husband were to take a concubine,' Hsiu-feng asked,
'would she have to be charming as well as beautiful?'

'Naturally,' said Yün.

From then on, Yün was obsessed with the idea of finding me a
concubine, even though we had nowhere near enough money for
such an ambition.

There was a courtesan from Chekiang named Wen Leng-hsiang
then living in Soochow. She was something of a poet, and had
written four stanzas on the theme of willow catkins that had taken
the city by storm, many talented writers composing couplets in
response to her originals. My friend from Wuchiang, Chang Hsien-

han, had long admired Leng-hsiang, and asked us to help him write some verses to accompany hers. Yün thought little of her and so declined, but I longed to write, and thus composed some verses to her rhyme. One couplet that Yün liked very much was, 'They arouse my springtime wistfulness, and ensnare her wandering fancy.'

A year later, on the 5th day of the eighth month, mother was planning to take Yün on a visit to Tiger Hill,[42] when my friend Hsien-han suddenly arrived at our house. 'I am going to Tiger Hill too,' he said, 'and today I came especially to invite you to go with me and admire some flowers[43] along the way.'

I then asked mother to go on ahead, and said I would meet her at Pantang near Tiger Hill. Hsien-han took me to Leng-hsiang's home, where I discovered that she was already middle-aged.

However, she had a daughter named Han-yüan, who, though not yet fully mature, was as beautiful as a piece of jade. Her eyes were as lovely as the surface of an autumn pond, and while they entertained us it became obvious that her literary knowledge was extensive. She had a younger sister named Wen-yüan who was still quite small.

At first I had no wild ideas and wanted only to have a cup of wine and chat with them. I well knew that a poor scholar like myself could not afford this sort of thing, and once inside I began to feel quite nervous. While I did not show my unease in my conversation, I did quietly say to Hsien-han 'I'm only a poor fellow. How can you invite these girls to entertain me?'

Hsien-han laughed. 'It's not that way at all. A friend of mine had invited me to come and be entertained by Han-yüan today, but then he was called away by an important visitor. He asked me to be the host and invite someone else. Don't worry about it.'

At that, I began to relax. Later, when our boat reached Pantang, I told Han-yüan to go aboard my mother's boat and pay her respects. That was when Yün met Han-yüan and, as happy as old friends at a reunion, they soon set off hand in hand to climb the hill in search of all the scenic spots it offered. Yün especially liked the height and vista of Thousand Clouds, and they sat there enjoying the view for some time. When we returned to Yehfangpin, we moored the boats side by side and drank long and happily.

As the boats were being unmoored, Yün asked me if Han-yüan could return aboard hers, while I went back with Hsien-han. To this, I agreed. When we returned to the Tuting Bridge we went back aboard our own boats and took leave of one another. By the time we arrived home it was already the third night watch.

'Today I have met someone who is both beautiful and charming,' said Yün. 'I have just invited Han-yüan to come and see me to-morrow, so I can try to arrange things for you.'

'But we're not a rich family,' I said, worried. 'We cannot afford to keep someone like that. How could people as poor as ourselves dare think of such a thing? And we are so happily married, why should we look for someone else?'

'But I love her too,' Yün said, laughing. 'You just let me take care of everything.'

The next day at noon, Han-yüan actually came. Yün entertained her warmly, and during the meal we played a game – the winner would read a poem, while the loser had to drink a cup of wine. By the end of the meal still not a word had been said about our obtaining Han-yüan.

As soon as she left, Yün said to me, 'I have just made a secret agreement with her. She will come here on the 18th, and we will pledge ourselves as sisters. You will have to prepare animals for the sacrifice.'

Then, laughing and pointing to the jade bracelet on her arm, she said, 'If you see this bracelet on Han-yüan's arm then, it will mean she has agreed to our proposal. I have just told her my idea, but I am still not very sure what she thinks about it all.'

I only listened to what she said, making no reply.

It rained very hard on the 18th, but Han-yüan came all the same. She and Yün went into another room and were alone there for some time. They were holding hands when they emerged, and Han-yüan looked at me shyly. She was wearing the jade bracelet!

We had intended, after the incense was burned and they had become sisters, that we should carry on drinking. As it turned out, however, Han-yüan had promised to go on a trip to Stone Lake, so she left as soon as the ceremony was over.

'She has agreed,' Yün told me happily. 'Now, how will you

reward your go-between?' I asked her the details of the arrangement.

'Just now I spoke to her privately because I was afraid she might have another attachment. When she said she did not, I asked her, "Do you know why we have invited you here today, little sister?"

' "The respect of an honourable lady like yourself makes me feel like a small weed leaning up against a great tree," she replied, "but my mother has high hopes for me, and I'm afraid I cannot agree without consulting her. I do hope, though, that you and I can think of a way to work things out."

'When I took off the bracelet and put it on her arm I said to her, "The jade of this bracelet is hard and represents the constancy of our pledge; and like our pledge, the circle of the bracelet has no end. Wear it as the first token of our understanding." To which she replied, "The power to unite us rests entirely with you." So it seems as if we have already won over Han-yüan. The difficult part will be convincing her mother, but I will think of a plan for that.'

I laughed, and asked her, 'Are you trying to imitate Li-weng's *Pitying the Fragrant Companion?*'[44]

'Yes,' she replied.

From that time on there was not a day that Yün did not talk about Han-yüan. But later Han-yüan was taken off by a powerful man, and all the plans came to nothing. In fact, it was because of this that Yün died.

PART II

The Pleasures of Leisure

When I was small I could stare directly at the sun with my eyes wide open. I could see the smallest things clearly and often took an almost mystic pleasure in making out the patterns on them.

During the summer, whenever I heard the sound of mosquitoes swarming, I would pretend they were a flock of cranes dancing across the open sky, and in my imagination they actually would become hundreds of cranes. I would look at them so long my neck became stiff. At night I would let mosquitoes inside my mosquito netting, blow smoke at them, and imagine that what I saw were white cranes soaring through blue clouds. It really did look like cranes flying among the clouds, and it was a sight that delighted me.

I would often squat down by unkempt grassy places in flower beds or by niches in walls, low enough so that my head was level with them, and concentrate so carefully that to me the grass became a forest and the insects became animals. Imagining that small mounds of earth were hills and that shallow holes were valleys, I let my spirit wander there in happiness and contentment.

Once while I was concentrating all my attention on two insects battling in the grass, a giant suddenly appeared, knocking down the mountains and pulling up the trees. It was nothing but a toad, but with one flick of his tongue he swallowed both the insects. I was small, and because I had been so caught up in the scene I could not help being frightened. When I had calmed down, I caught the toad, spanked it severely, and expelled it to a neighbour's yard. Since growing up I have sometimes thought that the battle of the two insects was probably an attempted rape. The ancients said, 'Rapists deserve death.' I wonder, was this why the insects were eaten by the toad?

One day while I was absorbed in my imaginary world, my egg

was bitten by an earthworm (in Soochow we call the male organs eggs), so that it swelled up and I could not urinate. The servants caught a duck, and were forcing it to open its mouth over the wound,[1] when suddenly one of them let go of the bird. The duck stretched out its neck as if to bite me there, and I screamed with fright. This became a family joke. These were all things that happened to me when I was small.

When I was a little older I became obsessed with a love of flowers, and found much delight in pruning miniature potted trees to make them look like real ones. It was not until I met Chang Lan-po, however, that I began really to learn how to prune branches and care for sprouts, and later to understand grafting and the creation of miniature rock formations in the pots. My favourite flower was the orchid, because of its elegant fragrance and charming appearance, though it is difficult to obtain ones that can be considered truly classic.

Shortly before Lan-po died he presented me with a pot of orchids that looked like lotus flowers. The centres were white and broad, and the edges of the petals were straight. They had thin stems, and the petals themselves were quite pale. This was a classic flower, and I treasured mine like a piece of old jade. When I was away from home Yün would water it herself, and its flowers and leaves grew luxuriantly. After I had had it for almost two years, however, it suddenly dried up and died. I dug it up and found the roots in good condition, white as jade with many new shoots. At first I could not understand it, and could only sigh at the thought that I was simply not lucky enough to raise so fine a flower. Only later did I learn that someone who had asked for a cutting and been refused had poured boiling water over it and killed it. I swore that from that time on I would never grow orchids again.

My next favourite flower was the azalea. Although it has no fragrance to speak of, its colours are long-lasting and it is easy to prune. But because Yün loved their branches and leaves, she could not stand seeing me prune them too much, so it was difficult to raise them properly. It was the same with all my other plants.

Every year chrysanthemums would grow east of the fence, blooming in the autumn. I preferred to pick them and put them in vases, rather than raise them in pots. It was not that I did not enjoy looking at them in pots, but because our house had no garden I could not grow them in pots myself, and had I bought them in the market and transplanted them, they would have looked all jumbled and wrong. I did not want that.

When putting chrysanthemums in a vase one should select an odd number of flowers, not an even number. Each vase should contain flowers of only a single colour. The mouths of the vases should be wide so that the flowers can spread out naturally.

Whether one is displaying five or seven flowers, or thirty or forty flowers, they should rise straight from the mouth of the vase in one mass, neither crowded together nor falling around loosely and leaning against the mouth of the vase. This technique is called 'rising tightly'.

Some of the flowers should stand up gracefully, while others spread out at angles. Some should be high and some low, with a few buds in between, to keep the arrangement from looking stiff and unnatural.

The leaves should not be disorderly and the stems should not be stiff. If one uses pins to hold the flowers in position they should be hidden, the long pins cut off so that none protrude from the stems. This technique is called 'clearing the mouth of the vase'.

From three to seven vases can be arranged on a table, depending on its size. No more than seven vases should be set out on one table, or it will not be possible to tell the eyes from the eyebrows, and the arrangement will look just like the cheap chrysanthemum screens sold in the markets. The stands should be from three or four inches to two feet and five or six inches tall. They should be different in height, but should be in proportion to one another so that there is an attractive relationship between the appearance of them all. If there is a tall stand in the centre with two low ones at the sides, or if the ones at the back are tall and the ones in front are low, or if they are set out in pairs, they will look like what people call a 'beautiful pile of trash'. Whether the flowers should be dense or spread out, whether they should lean towards the viewer or away, all depends on the sense of pictorial composition of someone who knows how to appreciate them.

When preparing flower pots, one can make a glue by mixing pitch, resin, elm bark, flour, and oil, and heating the mixture in the glowing ashes of rice stalks. Push pins up through a copper disc, and then heat the glue and stick the disc to the inside of the pot. After the glue has cooled, tie up a bunch of flowers with thin wire and push them down on to the pins. They should be at an angle to look best, and they should not be right in the middle of the pot. The branches should be separated, the leaves should stand out clearly, and the flowers themselves must not crowd together. Afterwards add water to the pot, and use a little sand to cover up the copper disc. The arrangement will only be correct if it looks as if the flowers have been grown in the pot.

To prune flowers picked from trees and fruits for display in a vase (for one cannot pick all the flowers oneself, and those picked by others will always be unsatisfactory), first hold them in your hand and turn them this way and that, to see how they look best. After deciding that, prune off the extra branches to make an attractive arrangement that is spare and uncommon. Then consider how the stems will curve when put into the vase, so that you can avoid having all the leaves at the back of the arrangement, or all the flowers at the sides. If you just take any branch that comes to hand and cut a straight stem from it to put into a vase, it will look stiff and out of place, the blooms will face sideways and the leaves will turn backwards so that the whole will be unattractive and inharmonious as well.

This is how to make a curve in a straight stem: saw halfway through it, insert a small piece of brick or stone into the cut, and the stem will bend. If the stem then tends to fall over, use one or two pins to strengthen it.

Even maple leaves and bamboo branches, bits of grass and thistles, can all be used in decorative arrangements. A single green bamboo twig – if complemented by a few aspen seeds, some leaves of fine grass, and two thistle branches, all of them in proper arrangement – can have an unworldly beauty.

When flowers and trees are planted for the first time, it does not matter if they are set in at an angle. Let the leaves face where they will, for after a year they and the branches will straighten up by themselves. In fact, if a tree is planted straight up it will be difficult for it to grow into a striking shape.

In raising potted trees, first select those which have roots that are exposed and crooked like chickens' feet. Cut off about the first three branches, then let the others grow. Each branch should have a section of the trunk to itself, with from seven to nine branches to the top of the tree. There should not be two branches opposite one another like shoulders, nor should the joints be swollen like the knees of a crane. The branches should grow out in all directions, not only to the right and left, or to the front and back, otherwise the tree will look bare. Some trees are called 'double-trunked' or 'triple-trunked'; this is when two or three trees grow from the same roots. If the roots of a tree do not look like chickens' feet the tree will look unattractive, as if it has been just stuck in the dirt.

The proper training of a tree takes at least thirty or forty years. In my lifetime I have seen only one man who managed to raise several trees properly, old Wan Tsai-chang of my home county. Once at a home in Yangchou I saw a potted boxwood and a potted cyprus that had been presented by a visitor from Yüshan, but this was at the home of a merchant and their being in such a place was as pitiful as brilliant pearls being thrown into the darkness. Other than these, the trees I have seen have not been particularly good. If the branches are allowed to grow out so that a tree looks like a pagoda, or if they twist around like earthworms, the tree will look as if it had been trained by only a common gardener.

While adding some detail in the pot with flowers or stones, try to create small scenes as lovely as pictures, or grand vistas of enchantment. These can be the delight of your study if you can lose yourself in contemplation of them when sitting with a cup of fine tea. Once when planting narcissi I had no stones from Lingpi[2] to put in the pot, so instead I used small pieces of coal that looked like stones. If one takes five or seven cabbage sprouts as white as jade and of various sizes, plants them in sand in a rectangular pot, and then covers the sand with small pieces of coal instead of stones, the black coal will contrast with the white cabbage and look most interesting. Thinking up possibilities like this can provide endless enjoyment, more than I can describe.

If one puts some calamus seeds in the mouth, chews them along with cold rice broth, and blows the mixture on to bits of charcoal which are then put in a dark and damp place, a very fine calamus will grow on them. The bits of charcoal can then be moved to a pot or a bowl, wherever one wants, and will look like stones covered with luxuriant moss.

Old lotus seeds can be ground off on each end and put into an eggshell, which can then be put with a chicken's other eggs and taken out when they hatch. Plant the seeds in a small pot using the mud from an old swallow's nest into which asparagus has been ground until it forms twenty per cent of the mixture. Water them with river water and let them get the light of the morning sun. When the flowers bloom they will be the size of a wine cup, and the leaves will have shrunk to the size of a bowl, a beautiful and charming effect.

In laying out gardens, pavilions, wandering paths, small mountains of stone, and flower plantings, try to give the feeling of the small in the large and the large in the small, of the real in the illusion, and of the illusion in the reality. Some things should be hidden and some should be obvious, some prominent and some vague. Arranging a proper garden is not just a matter of setting out winding paths in a broad area with many rocks; thinking that it is will only waste time and energy.

To make a miniature mountain, pile up some dirt, then place stones on it and plant flowers and grass here and there. The fence in front of it should be of plum trees, and the wall behind it should be covered with vines, so that it will look just like a mountain even though there is no mountain there.

This is a way of showing the small in the large: in an unused corner plant some bamboo, which will quickly grow tall, then plant some luxuriant plum trees in front to screen it.

This is a way to show the large in the small: the wall of a small garden should be winding and covered with green vines, and large stones decorated with inscriptions can be set into it.[3] Then one will be able to open a window and, while looking at a stone wall, feel as if one were gazing out across endless precipices.

Here is a way to show the real amidst an illusion: arrange the garden so that when a guest feels he has seen everything he can suddenly take a turn in the path and have a broad new vista open up before him, or open a simple door in a pavilion only to find it leads to an entirely new garden.

There are several ways of creating an illusion amidst reality: make a gateway into a closed yard, and then cover it over with bamboo and stones; the yard beyond, while real, will then look like an illusion. Or, on top of a wall build a low railing; it will look like an upper balcony, creating an illusion from reality.

Poor scholars who live in small crowded houses should re-arrange their rooms in imitation of the sterns of the Taiping boats of my home county, the steps of which can be made into three beds by extending them at front and back. Each bed is then separated from its neighbour by a board covered with paper. Looking at them when they are laid out is like walking a long road – you do not have a confined feeling at all. When Yün and I were living in Yangchou we arranged our house in this fashion. Though the house had only two spans,[4] we divided it into two bedrooms, a kitchen, and a living room, and still had plenty of space left over. Yün had laughed about our handiwork, saying, 'The layout is fine, but it still does not quite have the feel of a rich home.' I had had to admit she was right!

Once while I was sweeping the family graves in the mountains, I came across some pretty patterned stones, which I took home and talked over with Yün. 'If you use putty to set Hsüanchou[5] pebbles into a white stone pot,' I said, 'it looks attractive because the putty, the stones, and the pot are all the same colour. These yellow stones are lovely, but if I use the usual white putty on them it will contrast with the yellow of the stones and make the chisel marks on them stand out. What can I do about that?'

'Take the poorer stones,' said Yün, 'and pound them into dust. Mix the dust in with the putty and use it to fill in the chisel marks while it is still wet. When it dries perhaps the colours will be the same.'

We did as she suggested, and built up a miniature mountain in a rectangular pot from the kilns at Yihsing.[6] The mountain was on the left, with another small mound on the right. Along the mountain we made horizontal patterns, similar to those on the mountains in paintings by Yün-lin.[7] The cliffs were irregular, like those along a river bank. We filled an empty corner of the pot with river mud and planted duckweed, white with many petals. On top of the stones we planted morning glories, which are usually called cloud pines. It all took us several days to complete. By the deep autumn the morning glories had grown all over the mountain, covering it like wistaria hanging from a rock face, and when their flowers bloomed they were a deep red. The white duckweed also bloomed, and letting one's spirit wander among the red and the white was like a visit to Peng Island.[8] We put the pot out under the eaves and discussed it in great detail: here we should build a pavilion on the water, there a thatched arbour; here we should inscribe a stone with the characters 'Where flowers drop and waters flow'. We could live here, we could fish there, from this other place we could gaze off into the distance. We were as excited about it as if we were actually going to move to those imaginary hills and vales. But one night some miserable cats fighting over something to eat fell from the eaves, smashing the pot in an instant.

I sighed, and said, 'Even this little project has incurred the jealousy of heaven!' Neither of us could keep from shedding tears.

Burning incense in a quiet room is one of the refined pleasures of leisure. Yün used to take garu wood and other fragrant things and steam them in a rice cauldron. Then we would burn them slowly on a brass stand about half an inch above a fire; the scent was subtle and lovely, and there was no smoke. Buddha's Hands should not be smelled by someone who is drunk, or they will spoil.[9] Quinces should not be allowed to sweat; if they do, they should be washed with water. Only the *hsiangyüan*[10] does not need special treatment.

There are also ways of arranging Buddha's Hands and quinces as decorations, but I cannot write out the details of these. Often people will thoughtlessly pick up and smell something fragrant that is part of an arrangement, and then just as thoughtlessly put it back; these are people who do not understand decoration.

When living at home I always had a vase of flowers on my desk. Once Yün said to me, 'No matter what the weather, you can always manage to put together beautiful flower arrangements. Now in painting there is a school that specializes in insects on grasses. Why don't you try your hand at that?'

'There's no way to control the wandering of insects. How can I study them?' I answered.

'There is a way, but I am afraid it seems almost criminal to me,' said Yün.

'Try telling me.'

'When an insect dies its colours do not change,' Yün said. 'You could find an insect like a praying mantis, a cicada, or a butterfly, and kill it by sticking it with a pin. Then use a fine wire to tie its neck to a flower or a blade of grass, arranging its feet to grasp the stem or stand on a leaf. It will look just as if it were alive. Wouldn't that work?'

I was delighted and did as she suggested. No one who saw these insects failed to praise them. It is hard to find such clever women these days!

While Yün and I were staying with the Huas at Hsishan, Madam Hua had her two daughters learn characters from Yün. As they studied, the summer sun beat down with a fierce glare in the courtyard of their country home, so Yün showed them how to make movable screens out of live flowers. Each of these screens had a base made by taking two thin sticks of wood four or five inches long and joining them with four crosspieces each about a foot long, making a flat platform like the top of a low stool. Then she drilled round holes at each corner of this and stood a lattice of bamboo in them. In the middle she put a pot filled with sand and planted with hyacinth beans, the vines of which would climb up the bamboo lattice. The screens were about six or seven feet tall, but two people could easily move one of them. They can be put anywhere you like, filling the windows with green shade and blocking the sun while letting a breeze through. If you make several, they can be set out in winding patterns that can be rearranged as you like; thus they are called 'movable flower screens'. Any climbing vines or fragrant plants can be used to make them, and they render life in the countryside most pleasant.

My friend Lu Pan-fang, whose courtesy name was Chang and whose literary name was Chün-shan, was a talented painter of pine and cypress trees, and of plum flowers and chrysanthemums. He could also write in the li script[11] and inscribe chops. We once lived at his home, the Villa of Serenity, for a year and a half. The building we stayed in faced east and was of five spans, of which we occupied three. From our rooms we could gaze into the far distance, regardless of whether it was dark or bright, windy or rainy. In the yard there was a cassia tree with a lovely, clear fragrance, and the building itself had a hallway with side rooms, all very quiet.

When we moved there we took a servant couple with us, and they brought along their little daughter. The man could make clothes, and the woman could spin cotton; so to provide for our needs, Yün did embroidery, and the servant woman spun while her husband sewed.

I have always enjoyed entertaining, and for that we needed to buy a little wine for drinking games. Yün fortunately was good at making a meal without spending much money. Melon, vegetables, fish, and shrimps, when passed through Yün's hands, would take on a delicious taste. My friends knew I was poor, and they would often contribute some money for wine so that we could talk the day away. For my part, I kept the place spotless, and neither dominated the conversation nor objected to a casual atmosphere.

Among my friends were Yang Pu-fan, whose courtesy name was Chang-hsü and who was a talented portrait painter; Yüan Shao-yü, whose courtesy name was Pai and who was adept at painting mountains and rivers, and Wang Hsing-lan, whose courtesy name was Yen and who did skilful paintings of flowers and birds. They all liked the refined atmosphere at the Villa of Serenity, so they brought along their painting things and I studied with them. I would paint characters and carve chops, sell them, and give Yün the money so she could prepare tea and wine for our guests. We would spend the whole day doing nothing but criticizing poetry and talking about painting.

There were also the gentlemen Hsia Tan-an and his brother Yi-shan, Miao Shan-yi and his brother Chih-pai, and Chiang Yün-hsiang, Lu Chü-hsiang, Chou Hsiao-hsia, Kuo Hsiao-yü, Hua Hsin-fan, and Chang Hsien-han. They were like swallows on the rafters, coming and going as they pleased. Yün even sold her hairpins to buy wine without a second thought, because we did not want to give up lightly such a beautiful time and place.[12] But now we are all parted like clouds blown by the wind. The jade is broken, the incense buried![13] I cannot bear to look back.

Four things were forbidden at the Villa of Serenity: talking about official promotions, official business, or the eight-legged official examinations, and playing cards or dice. Offenders were fined five catties of wine.[14] Four things were encouraged: generosity, romantic refinement, an unrestrained atmosphere, and peace and quiet.

With nothing to do in the long summer, we held examination parties.[15] There would be eight people at each party, and each would bring two hundred copper cash. We would draw lots, and the winner would become the examination master, sitting apart and being in charge of the proceedings. The second would be the official recorder, and also sat separately. Everyone else became an examination candidate, and drew a sheet of paper from the recorder, all properly stamped with a seal. The examination master would announce two lines of poetry, one of five characters and one of seven characters, and the candidates would then have the time it took a stick of incense to burn in which to write lines rhyming with them. They could walk or stand while thinking, but no one was allowed to talk or exchange ideas. When they had finished their couplets they put them into a box, and were then allowed to sit down. To prevent favouritism, when everyone had handed in his paper the recorder opened the box and copied the papers into a book which he then gave to the examination master.[16]

From the sixteen[17] couplets, the best three of seven-character lines and the best three of five-character lines would be chosen. The writer of the couplet selected as the best of these six became the next examination master, and whoever was placed second would be the next recorder. Those who failed to have either of their couplets chosen would be fined twenty cash, and anyone who had no more than one chosen would be fined ten; if someone went beyond the time limit, he was fined forty. The examination master for each round got one hundred cash incense money,[18] so by playing ten rounds a day we would accumulate a thousand cash, enough for plenty of wine. Only Yün's was considered an official paper,[19] and she was allowed to sit while thinking out her answers.

One day Yang Pu-fan did a sketch of Yün and me in the garden;

it looked just like us. That night the moonlight was very beautiful, and the shadows the orchids sketched on the whitewashed wall were especially lovely. Hsing-lan was drunk, and merrily announced, 'Pu-fan can sketch your portrait, but I can paint the flowers' shadows.'

'But can you paint them as well as we were sketched?' I asked, laughing.

Hsing-lan then took a sheet of blank paper, put it up on the wall, and painted in the shadows with heavy and light ink, depending on whether they were dark or light as they were cast on the paper. We took it down and looked at it in the daylight, and while it could not be considered a true painting, he had captured the natural serenity of the leaves in the moonlight. Yün treasured it, and we all wrote inscriptions on it.

There were two places in Soochow, called the South Garden and the North Garden. We wanted to go there once when the rape flowers were in bloom, but unfortunately there were no wine houses near by where we could find something to drink. We could have taken a basket of things with us, but then we would have had to toast the flowers in cold wine and that would have been no fun at all.[20] We talked about looking for a drinking place near by, and about first looking at the flowers and then coming home to drink, but neither sounded as much fun as toasting the flowers with warm wine.

We had not made up our minds what to do when Yün laughed. 'Tomorrow all of you give me some wine money, and I'll bring a small stove myself.'

Everyone laughed and agreed.

After they left, I asked Yün, 'Are you really going to bring a stove yourself?'

'No,' she said, 'but in the market I've seen dumpling-sellers who carry with them a pan, a small stove, and everything else we might need. Why not hire one of them to go with us? I can cook the food beforehand, and we can warm things up when we get there.'

'That sounds fine for the wine and the food,' I said, 'but what are you going to do for a teapot?'

'We can take along an earthenware pot,' said Yün, 'hang it right over the little stove with an iron hook, and add some more fuel to heat the tea. Wouldn't that work?'

I clapped my hands in approval. There was a dumpling-seller named Pao on the street corner, and I offered him a hundred cash to bring his things with us the next afternoon. He happily agreed. The next day when all those who were going with us to look at the flowers had arrived, I told them what we had done and they all sighed with admiration.

After lunch we went off to the South Garden, carrying cushions and mats with us. We picked a place in the shade of a willow tree and sat down. First we made tea, and when we had finished it, we warmed the wine and cooked the food. The wind and sun were exquisite. The earth was golden, and the blue clothes and red sleeves of strollers filled the paths between the fields, while butter-flies and bees flew all around us. The scene was so intoxicating one hardly needed to drink. After a while the wine and food were ready, and everyone sat down on the ground to feast. The man who had helped us out was not an ordinary sort, so we persuaded him to come and join us in our drinking. The strollers who saw us all envied our clever idea. By the end of the afternoon cups and plates were scattered around and all of us were very jolly, some sitting and some lying down, some singing and some whistling. As the red sun set I felt like eating some rice porridge, so our helper quickly bought some rice and cooked it, and we all went home well satis-fied.

'Did you all enjoy today's trip?' asked Yün.

'Without your help it wouldn't have been nearly so much fun,' they replied. Laughing and joking, we parted.

Poor scholars should be frugal but still refined and clean insofar as their home, clothing, and food are concerned. I define frugality as 'knowing when to save money'.

For example, at meals I like a little to drink but do not enjoy a great many dishes. So Yün once made a plum flower tray, by taking six white porcelain saucers two inches across and putting one in the middle and the five others around the outside, so that when set together they looked like a plum flower. These she painted grey, and then made a cover for the tray that was rounded with a handle on top shaped like a flower stem. When placed on the table it looked as if a plum flower had been put there, and the food seemed to have been set down on its petals. One tray with six different dishes was enough for a leisurely meal with two or three close friends. If we ate everything, we would just refill the tray. Yün also made a round tray with a low edge on which she could conveniently put things like cups, chopsticks, and wine pots, making it easy to carry them around and set them down wherever she liked. These are all examples of frugality in eating.

Yün also made all my caps, collars, and socks. If clothes develop holes, they can be patched by using pieces of the same garment. They should look neat and clean. Clothes should be dark in colour so that dirty spots will not show; then they can be worn either to go out, or around the house. These are examples of frugality in clothing.

When we first moved to the Villa of Serenity we felt our rooms were too dark, so we pasted white paper on the walls to brighten them up. During the summer we took out the downstairs windows, but there were no screens and we felt the place was too open and lacking in privacy.

'There are those old bamboo curtains,' said Yün. 'Why don't we use them in place of screens?'

'How?' I asked.

'We could take several lengths of bamboo and paint them black,' she said, 'and make a framework out of them that fills the top of the window while leaving the lower half of it empty. Then cut one of the bamboo curtains in half and hang it from the framework so that it reaches down as far as a table top. Four short pieces of bamboo can be tied up vertically in the empty space, and finally we can cover the crosspiece from which the bamboo curtain is hung by winding strips of old black cloth around it and sewing them together. It would give us privacy, be attractive, and not cost anything.'

This is another example of what I mean by 'knowing when to save money'. One should apply this rule in everything. The saying of the ancients, 'Even ends of bamboo and sawdust have their uses', is very true.

When lotus flowers bloom in the summer, they close up at night but open again in the morning. Yün used to put a few tea leaves in a gauze bag and put it inside a lotus flower before it closed in the evening. The next morning she would take out the tea and boil it with natural spring water. It had a wonderful and unique fragrance.

PART III

The Sorrows of Misfortune

Why are there misfortunes in life? They are usually the retributions for one's own sins, but this was not so with me! I always have been friendly, frank, and open, and kept my word to others, but these qualities only became the reasons for my troubles. My father, the Honourable Chia-fu, was also a most generous gentleman, anxious to help those in trouble, to assist anyone in need, to marry off other people's daughters and to bring up their sons. There are countless examples. He spent money like dirt, most of it for other people.

When my wife and I were living at home, we could not avoid pawning our belongings if we had unforeseen expenses; at first we somehow found ways to make ends meet, but later we were always in need. As people say, 'Without money, you cannot both run a household and mix with friends.' First our circumstances aroused talk amongst local gossips, and later scorn from our family. The ancients were right: 'Lack of talent in a woman is a virtue.'

Although I was the eldest son in the family, I was the third child, and so at first everyone called Yün 'third lady'. Later, however, they suddenly started calling her 'third wife'. It began as a joke, but then became usual practice, so that everyone from the elders to the servants was calling her 'third wife'.[1] I wonder, was this the beginning of the disagreements in our family?

In 1785 I was working for my father at the Haining government offices.[2] Yün usually enclosed notes to me in letters from home, so one day my father said to me, 'Since your wife can handle brush and ink, she can write your mother's letters for her.' But sometime later there was some gossip at home, and mother suspected Yün of writing something improper about it in one of her letters. After that she did not let Yün take up the brush for her.

When father noticed that later letters were not in Yün's handwriting he asked me whether she was ill. I wrote and asked her about it, but Yün did not reply.

After a while father grew quite angry about this, and said to me, 'Apparently your wife will not condescend to write letters for your mother!' It was not until I returned home that I realized the cause of the misunderstanding, and I wanted to put things right for Yün.

She hurriedly stopped me, however, saying, 'I would rather have father blaming me for this than to have mother unhappy with me.' So things were not cleared up after all.

In the spring of 1790 I was again working for my father, at the secretariat at Hungchiang.[3] A colleague of my father's named Yü Fu-ting had brought along his family to live there with him.

One day my father said to Fu-ting, 'I have led a hard life, often away from home. I would like to have someone to live with me and serve me, but I have not been able to find anyone.[4] If my son respected my wishes he would find me someone from our home county so that our dialects would be the same.'

Fu-ting passed this on to me, and I secretly wrote to Yün telling her to find someone. She did, a girl named Yao. As father had at that time not yet accepted her, however, Yün decided it would be best not to tell my mother about what was going on. When the girl came for my father to meet her, Yün made up a story saying that she was a neighbour's daughter who was visiting. And when my father sent me to bring her formally from her home to his residence, Yün again listened to the advice of others and made up a story saying that my father had admired her for some time.

When mother learned what had happened she was outraged. 'But this is the neighbour's daughter who came for a visit,' she said. 'How can he marry her?' Yün had made mother angry with her too.

In the spring of 1792 I was living at Chenchou.[5] My father fell ill at Hungchiang and when I went to see him I was taken sick too. At that time my younger brother Chi-tang was working under my father.

While there I received a letter from Yün saying, 'Your younger brother Chi-tang once borrowed money from a lady neighbour and asked me to be the guarantor. Now she is anxious to have the money back.'

I asked Chi-tang about it, but he only said that Yün was meddling in his affairs. I merely replied at the end of a letter, 'Father and I are both ill, and we have no money to repay the loan. Wait until younger brother returns home and let him take care of it himself.'

Father and I recovered not long afterwards, and I returned to Chenchou. Yün's reply to my note arrived at Hungchiang after I had left, and father opened and read it. In her letter, Yün wrote of my younger brother's borrowing from the neighbour, and also said, 'Your mother thinks the old man's illness is all because of the Yao girl. When he is a bit better, you should secretly order Yao to write to her parents saying she is homesick. I will tell her parents to go to Yangchou to fetch her home. This way, both sides can disclaim responsibility for her departure.'

When my father read this he was furious. He asked Chi-tang about the loan from the neighbour, but Chi-tang said he knew nothing of it. Father then wrote a letter reprimanding me, in which he said, 'Your wife has borrowed money behind your back, and is now trying to say it is all little uncle's fault.[6] Moreover, she called her mother-in-law "your mother", and referred to me as "old man".[7] This is outrageous! I have already sent a messenger with a letter back to Soochow, ordering that she be expelled from the house. If you have any shame at all, you will recognize your errors!'

Receiving this letter was like hearing a clap of thunder on a clear day. I wrote a letter apologizing to father, and quickly rode home, afraid that Yün would commit suicide. I had arrived home and was explaining the whole affair when the servant arrived with father's letter, detailing Yün's errors in the harshest terms.

Yün wept and said, 'I may have been wrong to write so improperly, but father should forgive the ignorance of a woman.'

After a few days another letter arrived from my father saying, 'I am willing to relent a little. You may take your wife and live somewhere else. If I do not have to see your face I will not be so angry!'[8]

It was suggested that Yün go back to her home for a while, but her mother was dead and her younger brother had run away; and she did not want to go and depend on her other relatives. Fortunately my friend Lu Pan-fang heard about our situation and, sympathizing with us, invited us to go and live at his home, the Villa of Serenity. After we had spent two years there, father gradually came to realize what had happened. I had just returned from South-of-the-Mountains[9] when father himself came to the Villa of Serenity, told Yün he now understood what had happened, and invited us to return home.

This we did, happy at the reunion with our flesh and blood. Who would have guessed that the curse of Han-yüan still lay ahead?

Yün had had the blood sickness ever since her younger brother Ko-chang had run away from home and her mother had missed him so much that she died of grief. Yün was so distraught she had fallen ill herself. From the time she met Han-yüan, she passed no blood for over a year, and I was delighted that Yün had found such a good cure in her friend, when Han-yüan was snatched away by an influential man who paid a thousand golds[10] for her and also promised to take care of her mother. 'The beauty belongs to Sha-shih-li!'[11] I had learned of all this but had not dared to say anything to Yün, so she did not find out about it until one day when she went to see Han-yüan. She returned weeping, and said, 'I had not thought Han's feelings could be so shallow!'

'Your own feelings are too deep,' I said. 'How can that sort of person be said to have feelings? Someone who is used to beautiful clothes and delicate foods could never grow accustomed to thorn hairpins and plain cloth dresses. It's better that we should be unsuccessful now than to have her regret things later.'

I comforted her repeatedly, but having been so wounded Yün still suffered great discharges of blood. She was bedridden and did not respond to any treatment. She suffered relapses, and became so thin you could see her bones. After a few years the money we owed increased daily, and so did the gossip about us. And because she had pledged sisterhood with a sing-song girl, my parents' scorn for Yün deepened daily. I became the mediator between my parents and my wife. It was no way to live!

Yün had given birth to a girl named Ching-chün, who by then was fourteen years old. She could read and write well and was also very capable, so fortunately we could rely on her help in pawning hairpins and clothes.[12] Our son was named Feng-sen; at this time he was twelve years old and was studying reading with a teacher. I was then without employment for several years, so I had opened up a shop in our home, selling books and paintings. But I did not make enough in three days to pay the expenses of one. I was weary and beset by hardships, and we often had no money. In the deepest winter I had no furs, but there was nothing to do but to be strong and bear the cold. Ching-chün, too, shivered in an unlined dress, though she bravely denied being cold. On account of this, Yün swore she would never spend the money to see a doctor or buy medicine.

Once during a period when Yün was able to get out of bed, it happened that my friend Chou Chun-hsi had just returned from Prince Fu's secretariat and wanted to hire someone to embroider the Heart Sutra[13] for him. Yün thought that by embroidering a sutra she might bring us some luck to ease our difficulties, as well as getting a good price for her work, so despite her illness she agreed to do it. As it turned out Chun-hsi was only on a quick visit and could not wait long, needing the job completed in ten days. Yün was still weak, and the sudden work made her waist hurt and gave her dizzy spells. Who would have thought her fate was so bad that even the Buddha would not show her mercy! After she had embroidered the sutra, her illness worsened. First she would call for water, then she would want soup. The family began to grow weary of her.

There was a Westerner who had rented the house to the left of my painting shop. He made his living by lending out money at interest, and I had come to know him when he asked me to do paintings for him.[14] A friend of mine had once borrowed fifty golds from him, asking me to be the guarantor. I would have been embarrassed to refuse and so agreed to it, but then he ended up by running off with the loan. The Westerner had only me to ask for repayment, and often came to demand his money. At first I gave him paintings in lieu of payment, but gradually I came to have nothing left to give him. At the end of the year while my father was at home, he came again to demand repayment, and made a commotion at the gate.

When my father heard the noise he called for me and scolded me angrily, saying, 'We are a house of robes and caps.¹⁵ How could we owe money to someone like this!'

Just as I was about to explain, a messenger arrived. He had been sent by a woman who had been a sworn sister of Yün's as a child, who had married a man named Hua from Hsishan, and who had heard of her illness and wanted to inquire after her.

My father, however, mistakenly thought he was a messenger from Han-yüan and so became even angrier, saying, 'Your wife does not behave as a woman should, swearing sisterhood with a sing-song girl. Nor do you think to learn from your elders, running around with riff-raff. I cannot bear to send you to the execution ground, but I will give you only three days. Make plans to leave home, and make them quickly. If you take longer, you will lose your head for your disobedience!'¹⁶

When Yün heard this she wept, and said, 'It is all my fault that father is so angry. Yet if I committed suicide and you left home, you could not bear it; and if I stayed here while you left, you could not stand it. Go secretly and tell the messenger from the Huas to come here. I will force myself to get out of bed and talk to him.'

I told Ching-chün to help her out of the bedroom, and fetched the messenger from the Huas. 'Did your mistress send you here specially,' Yün asked, 'or did you come because you just happened to be passing this way?'

The messenger replied, 'My mistress had heard of madam's illness some time ago, and originally wanted to come personally to visit you. But because she had never entered your gate before, she did not dare to come herself. As I was leaving she told me to say that if madam does not mind a plain and rustic life, she could come and build up her strength in the countryside, according to the pledge they made to one another under the lamplight when they were young.' This last referred to a pledge Yün and she had made once when they were embroidering together, to help one another if they were ever ill.

So Yün told him to go home quickly and ask his mistress to send a boat for us secretly two days later.

After he left, Yün said to me, 'Sister Hua is closer to me than my own flesh and blood. If you don't mind moving to her home, we can go there together. I'm afraid we won't be able to take the children with us, though, and we certainly cannot leave them here to trouble our parents. We will have to make arrangements for them in the next two days.'

At that time my cousin Wang Chin-chen had a son named Yün-shih and wanted to have Ching-chün for his daughter-in-law. 'I hear young Wang is timid and without much ability,' said Yün, 'and that while he will be able to keep up what the Wangs own, they do not own much to keep up. On the other hand, they are a respectable family and have only the one son.[17] I think we should allow the marriage.'

I met with Chin-chen and said, 'My father and you have the friendship of Weiyang.[18] If you want Ching-chün for your daughter-in-law I do not think he will refuse you. But she must be brought up a little longer before she is ready for marriage, and in the circumstances we will not be able to do that. After my wife and I have gone to Hsishan, how would you feel about going to my parents and asking for her first to be your child daughter-in-law?'[19] He happily agreed to my suggestion.

I also made arrangements for our son Feng-sen, asking my friend Hsia Yi-shan to introduce him to someone from whom he could learn the business of trading. This was no sooner done than the Huas' boat arrived. It was then the 25th day of the twelfth month of 1800.

Yün said to me, 'Since we are leaving alone, I am afraid that not only will the neighbours laugh at us, but also that the Westerner will not let us go as we still cannot repay his loan. We must go quietly tomorrow morning at the fifth night watch.'[20]

'But you are ill,' I protested. 'Can you stand the morning cold?'

'Life and death are governed by fate,' Yün replied. 'Do not worry about me.'

I secretly informed my father of what we were going to do, and he agreed to it. That night I first carried a little baggage down to the boat on a shoulder pole, and then told Feng-sen to go to sleep. Ching-chün was crying at her mother's side.

These were Yün's parting instructions to our daughter: 'Your mother has had a bitter fate and emotions that run too deep;

therefore we have had these many problems. Fortunately your father has been kind to me, and there is nothing to worry about in our leaving. In two or three years we will be able to arrange for us all to be reunited. Go to your new home, behave as a proper woman in everything you do, and do not be like your mother. Your father-in-law and mother-in-law will be happy to have you, and will surely treat you well. You can take with you all the cases, boxes, and anything else we have left behind. Your little brother is still young, so we have not told him what we are doing. When we are about to leave, we will tell him that I am going to see a doctor and will be back in a few days; after we have left, explain everything to him, and let grandfather take care of him.'

At our side was the old woman who had once rented us her house so that we could escape the summer's heat. She wanted to go with us to the countryside, and since she could not she stood beside us wiping away her tears. Just before the striking of the fifth night watch we all ate some warm rice porridge.

Yün laughed bravely. 'Once it was rice porridge that brought us together,' she said, 'and now it is rice porridge that sends us away. If someone wrote a play about it, he could call it *The Romance of the Rice Porridge.*'

Feng-sen heard her talking and woke up, saying sleepily, 'What are you doing, mother?'

'I am going out to see a doctor,' Yün replied.

'Why so early?'

'Because it is far away. You and elder sister should stay home and be good. Do not make grandmother angry. I am going with your father and will be back in a few days.'

As the cock crowed three times, Yün, with tears in her eyes and her arm around the old woman, was just opening the back door to go out when Feng-sen cried loudly, 'Yi! My mother is not coming back!'

Ching-chün feared he would awaken others, so she quickly covered his mouth with her hand and comforted him. By this time Yün and I felt as if we were being torn apart, but there was nothing more we could say. We could only tell him not to cry.

After Ching-chün shut the door, Yün was able to walk only

about a dozen steps from our lane before she was too tired to go any farther. We continued with me carrying Yün on my back and the old woman holding up the lantern. We had nearly reached the boat when we were almost arrested by a night patrolman, but fortunately the servant woman told him that Yün was her daughter who was ill and that I was her son-in-law. When the boatmen (who all worked for the Hua family) heard us talking, they came to meet us and helped us down to the boat. After we cast off Yün finally burst out crying, and wept bitterly. After this separation, mother and son never saw each other again.

Hua was named Ta-cheng, and he lived facing the mountains at Tungkaoshan in Wuhsi.[21] He farmed the land himself, and was very simple and sincere. His wife – Yün's sworn sister – was from the Hsia family. It was early in the afternoon of that day before we arrived at their house. Madam Hua had been waiting for us by the gate, and when we arrived she led her two small daughters to the boat to greet us. Everyone was very happy to see us. Yün was helped ashore and we were treated very hospitably. After a while the neighbours' wives burst into the room along with their children, and stood around Yün looking her over. Some asked her questions, some offered her condolences, while others whispered to one another, all filling the house with the sound of their chatter.

Yün told Madam Hua, 'Today I feel just like the fisherman who wandered into Peach Blossom Spring!'[22]

'Please don't laugh at our country folk,' replied Mrs Hua. 'That which they seldom see they consider most wonderful.'[23]

Thus we settled down to pass the New Year. Only two score days after we arrived, by the Festival of the First Moon, Yün was starting to be able to get up and around. That night as we watched the dragon lanterns on the threshing floor, her spirits began to revive. I then began to feel at peace myself, and decided to talk our situation over with her. 'We have no future living here,' I said, 'but we are too short of money to go anywhere else. What do you think we should do?'

'I have been thinking about this too,' said Yün. 'Your elder sister's husband Fan Hui-lai is now chief accountant at the Ching-chiang Salt Office. Ten years ago when he wanted to borrow ten golds from you we did not have the money and I pawned my hairpins to get it. Do you remember?'

'I had forgotten!'

'I hear Chingchiang is not far away. Why don't you go and see if he can help us?'

I did as she suggested. At the time it was very warm, and I felt the heat even dressed only in a woollen gown and a worsted short jacket. This was the 16th day of the first month of 1801. That night I spent at an inn at Hsishan, where I rented bedding.

The next morning I took a boat for Chiangyin, but the winds were against us and there was a continuous drizzle. By the time we reached the river mouth at Chiangyin the spring cold was cutting me to the bone. I bought some wine to ward off the cold, but that exhausted my purse. All night I tried to decide whether I should sell my undergarments to get money for the ferry.[24]

By the 19th the north wind was stronger and the snow was deeper everywhere. I could not hold back bitter tears. Alone, I worked out lodging and ferry expenses, and did not dare to buy any more to drink. I was trembling in soul and body when an old man suddenly entered the inn, wearing straw sandals and a felt hat and carrying a yellow bag on his back. He looked at me as if he knew me.

'Aren't you Tsao from Taichou?' I asked.

'I am,' he replied, 'and if it were not for you I would be lying dead in a ditch by now! My little girl is well, and she often sings your praises. What a surprise to meet you today! What are you hanging about here for?'

Now when I was working in the government offices at Taichou[25] there was this same Tsao, a poor man with a beautiful daughter who had already been betrothed. But then a man of some influence had loaned him money in a plan to obtain his daughter, and it had all led to legal proceedings. I had helped protect them and send his daughter back to her betrothed. In his gratitude, Tsao had volunteered as a servant at the *yamen* and kowtowed to me, and so I had come to know him. I told him how I had been going to see my brother-in-law and had run into the snowstorm.

'I am heading that way myself,' Tsao said. 'If the weather clears tomorrow I will take you there.' Then he took out money to buy wine, and was most courteous to me.

On the 20th, as soon as the monastery's morning bells began to ring, I heard the ferryman's shouts by the river mouth. I got up in a hurry and called to Tsao to come along. 'Don't be in such a rush,' he said. 'We should eat our fill before boarding the boat.'

Then he paid for my room and my meals, and took me off to buy something for breakfast. I had been delayed for days, and was anxious to get across on the ferry, so I did not feel like eating, but I forced down two sesame cakes. As we boarded the boat, the river wind cut through our garments like an arrow, and soon I was trembling in all four limbs.

'I hear a Chiangyin man has hung himself in Chingchiang,' said Tsao, 'and that his wife has chartered this boat to go there. We have to wait for her before we can cross.' I had to wait until noon before we cast off, still hungry and fighting the cold. By the time we reached Chingchiang the smoke from evening cooking fires was rising on all sides.

'There are two *yamen* at Chingchiang,' said Tsao.[26] 'Is the man you are visiting at the one inside the wall or the one outside the wall?'

Staggering along behind him, I confessed I did not know. 'Then we might just as well stop here for the night,' Tsao said, 'and go to look for him tomorrow.'

My shoes and stockings were filthy with mud and wet through, so at the inn that night I asked to dry them by the fire. I gulped down a meal and fell into an exhausted sleep, however, so that by the time I awoke the next day my stockings were half burned.

That morning Tsao once again paid for my room and board. We arrived at the *yamen* inside the wall to find that Hui-lai had not yet got up, but on hearing that I had arrived he threw on some clothes and came out. Seeing the state I was in, he was very upset; 'What calamity has brought you here?' he asked.

'Just a moment,' I said. 'First, have you got two golds you can loan me to repay the man who brought me here?'

Hui-lai gave me two barbarian cakes,[27] and I offered them to Tsao. He was determined to refuse them, but finally accepted one and left. I then told Hui-lai everything that had happened, and why I had come.

'You and I are relatives by marriage,' he said, 'and even if there were no old debt I should do everything I could for you. But unfortunately our sea-going salt boats have just been taken by pirates. We are now trying to straighten out the accounts, and I have no means of finding the money. The best I could do would be to give you twenty coins of barbarian silver to repay the debt. Would that be all right?'

I had not had any extravagant hopes to begin with, so I accepted. I stayed on two more days, but when the sky cleared and the weather turned warmer I made plans to go back, returning to the Huas on the 25th.

Yün asked whether I had run into the snow, and I told her about my ordeal. 'When it snowed I thought you had already reached Chingchiang,' she said sadly, 'but you were still held up at the river mouth. You were lucky to run into old Tsao. It's true that heaven watches over the good.'

Several days later we received a letter from Ching-chün telling us that Yi-shan had already found Feng-sen a job in a shop. Chin-chen had asked permission of my father and on the 24th day of the first month had taken Ching-chün to his home. Our children's affairs seemed well in order, but we were still sad at being parted from them.

By the beginning of the second month the sun was warmer and the wind less strong, and with the money I had got at Chingchiang I made some simple preparations to visit my old friend Hu Ken-tang at the Hanchiang[28] Salt Bureau. There was a tax office there, where I succeeded in obtaining a position as secretary, after which body and soul were a little more settled.[29]

In the eighth month of the next year, 1802, I received a letter from Yün saying, 'My illness is now completely cured. I don't think it is a good idea for me to live and board indefinitely at a home where I have neither relatives nor friends. I would like to join you at Hanchiang, and see the glory of Ping Mountain.'

After receiving this letter I rented a house of two spans facing the river outside the Hsienchun Gate at Hanchiang, and went myself to the Huas to fetch Yün. Madam Hua presented us with a child servant called Ah Shuang, to help with housework and meals, and we agreed that one day we should all be neighbours. By this time it was already the tenth month, and bitterly cold on Ping Mountain, so Yün and I decided not to go there until spring.

With Yün recovered we were happy again, and full of hope that we could reunite our family. But before the month was out the tax bureau suddenly cut its staff by fifteen persons, and as I was only the friend of a friend, I was dismissed. At first Yün still managed to come up with a hundred plans for us, putting on a brave front to comfort me. Never did she in the least find fault, though by the second month of spring, 1803, she began to suffer great discharges of blood once again. I wanted to return to Chingchiang and beg my brother-in-law for more help, but, as Yün put it, 'It's better to ask for help from a friend than from a relative.'

'That's true,' I replied, 'but all our friends are now out of work as well. While they may be concerned about us, they could not help us if they wanted to.'

'Then fortunately the weather at least has turned warm,' said Yün, 'so you won't have to worry about the road being blocked by snow. Please go quickly, come back as soon as you can, and don't worry about my being ill. If anything were to happen to you, my sins would be even heavier.'

Our income was irregular, but so that Yün would not worry I pretended to her that I was hiring a mule. In fact I walked, with some cakes in my bag and eating as I went. I headed south-east for about eighty or ninety *li*, twice taking a ferry across a forked river, and finally coming to a district where I could see no villages in any direction. I walked on until it grew late, but still saw only endless stretches of yellow sand and bright, twinkling stars. Finally I came to an earth god shrine, about five feet tall and surrounded by a low wall. A pair of cypress trees was planted beside it.

I kowtowed to the god and said a prayer. 'My name is Shen and I am from Soochow. I am going to visit relatives, but have lost my way. Let me borrow your temple for a night's rest. Blessed spirit, protect me.'

I then moved aside the small stone incense pot and squeezed

myself into the shrine. It was big enough for only half my body, so I turned my wind cap around to cover my face and lay half inside the shrine with my knees sticking out. I shut my eyes and listened quietly, but the only sound was the whistling of the wind. With my feet tired and my spirits weak, I collapsed into sleep.

When I awoke it was already light in the east, and suddenly I heard the sound of walking and talking outside the wall. I rushed out to see who it was, and it turned out to be some local people passing by on their way to market. I asked the way to Chingchiang, and one of them told me, 'Go south ten *li* and you will come to the county seat at Taihsing City. Go straight through the town and then head east for another ten *li*, when you will come to an earthen mound. Pass eight of these mounds and you will come to Chingchiang. All these places are along the main road.'

I went back inside the shrine to return the incense pot to its original position, then kowtowed my thanks to the god and left. After passing through Taihsing I was able to take a wheelbarrow,[30] and arrived at Chingchiang about four o'clock in the afternoon. I sent my calling card in to my brother-in-law's office, but only after a long while did the gate-keeper come out and tell me, 'His Honour Mr Fan has gone to Changchou on business.'

From the way he spoke, this sounded like an excuse. 'When will he be back?' I asked.

'I don't know.'

'Then I will wait for him,' I said, 'even if I have to wait a year.'

The gate-keeper saw that I meant what I said, and quietly asked me, 'Is His Honour Mr Fan's mother-in-law really your mother?'

'If she were not, I would not be waiting for Mr Fan to come back!'

'Then you just wait for him,' the gate-keeper said. After three days I was told Hui-lai had returned, and was given twenty-five golds. I hired a mule and hurried home.

I returned to find Yün moaning and weeping, looking as if something awful had happened. As soon as she saw me she burst out, 'Did you know that yesterday noon Ah Shuang stole all our things and ran away? I have asked people to search everywhere, but they still have not found him. Losing our things is a small matter, but what of our relationship with our friends? As we were leaving, his mother told me over and over again to take good care of him. I'm terribly worried he's running back home and will have to cross the Great River.[31] And what will we do if his parents have hidden him to blackmail us?[32] How can I face my sworn sister again?'

'Please calm down,' I said. 'You've been worrying about it too much. You can only blackmail someone who has money; with you and me, it's all our four shoulders can do to support our two mouths. Besides, in the half year the boy has been with us, we have given him clothing and shared our food with him. Our neighbours all know we have never once beaten him or scolded him. What's really happened is that the wretched child has ignored his conscience and taken advantage of our problems to run away with our belongings. Your sworn sister at the Huas' gave us a thief. How can you say you cannot face her? It is she who should not be able to face you. What we should do now is report this case to the magistrate, so as to avoid any questions being raised about it in the future.'

After Yün heard me speak, her mind seemed somewhat eased, but from then on she began frequently to talk in her sleep, calling out, 'Ah Shuang has run away!' or 'How could Han-yüan turn her back on me?' Her illness worsened daily.

Finally I was about to call a doctor to treat her, but she stopped me. 'My illness began because of my terribly deep grief over my brother's running away and my mother's death,' said Yün. 'It continued because of my affections, and now it has returned because of my indignation. I have always worried too much about things, and while I have tried my best to be a good daughter-in-law, I have failed.

'These are the reasons why I have come down with dizziness and palpitations of the heart. The disease has already entered my vitals, and there is nothing a doctor can do about it. Please do not spend money on something that cannot help.

'I have been happy as your wife these twenty-three years. You have loved me and sympathized with me in everything, and never rejected me despite my faults. Having had for my husband an intimate friend like you, I have no regrets over this life. I have had warm cotton clothes, enough to eat, and a pleasant home. I have strolled among streams and rocks, at places like the Pavilion of the Waves and the Villa of Serenity. In the midst of life, I have been just like an Immortal. But a true Immortal must go through many incarnations before reaching enlightenment. Who could dare hope to become an Immortal in only one lifetime? In our eagerness for immortality, we have only incurred the wrath of the Creator, and brought on our troubles with our passion. Because you have loved me too much, I have had a short life!'

Later she sobbed and spoke again. 'Even someone who lives a hundred years must still die one day. I am only sorry at having to leave you so suddenly and for so long, halfway through our journey. I will not be able to serve you for all your life, or to see Feng-sen's wedding with my own eyes.' When she finished, she wept great tears.

I forced myself to be strong and comforted her saying, 'You have been ill for eight years, and it has seemed critical many times. Why do you suddenly say such heartbreaking things now?'

'I have been dreaming every night that my parents have sent a boat to fetch me,' said Yün. 'When I shut my eyes it feels as if I'm floating, as if I were walking in the mist. Is my spirit leaving me, while only my body remains?'

'That is only because you are upset,' I said. 'If you will relax, drink some medicine, and take care of yourself, you will get better.'

Yün only sobbed again and said, 'If I thought I had the slightest thread of life left in me I would never dare alarm you by talking to you like this. But the road to the next world is near, and if I do not speak to you now there will never be a day when I can.

'It is all because of me that you have lost the affection of your parents and drifted apart from them. Do not worry, for after I die you will be able to regain their hearts. Your parents' springs and autumns are many, and when I die you should return to them quickly. If you cannot take my bones home, it does not matter if you leave my coffin here for a while until you can come for it. I also want you to find someone who is attractive and capable, to serve our parents and bring up my children. If you will do this for me, I can die in peace.'

When she had said this a great sad moan forced itself from her, as if she was in an agony of heartbreak.

'If you part from me half way I would never want to take another wife,' I said. 'You know the saying, "One who has seen the ocean cannot desire a stream, and compared with Wu Mountain there are no clouds anywhere." '[33]

Yün then took my hand and it seemed there was something else she wanted to say, but she could only brokenly repeat the two words 'next life'. Suddenly she fell silent and began to pant, her eyes staring into the distance. I called her name a thousand times, but she could not speak. Two streams of agonized tears flowed from her eyes in torrents, until finally her panting grew shallow and her tears dried up. Her spirit vanished in the mist and she began her long journey. This was on the 30th day of the third month in the 7th year of the reign of the Emperor Chia Ching.[34] When it happened there was a solitary lamp burning in the room. I looked up but saw nothing, there was nothing for my two hands to hold, and my heart felt as if it would shatter. How can there be anything greater than my everlasting grief?

My friend Hu Ken-tang loaned me ten golds, and by selling every single thing remaining in the house I put together enough money to give my beloved a proper burial.

Alas! Yün came to this world a woman, but she had the feelings and abilities of a man. After she entered the gate of my home in marriage, I had to rush about daily to earn our clothing and food, there was never enough, but she never once complained. When I was living at home, all we had for entertainment was talk about literature. What a pity that she should have died in poverty and after long illness. And whose fault was it that she did? It was my fault, what else can I say? I would advise all the husbands and wives in the world not to hate one another, certainly, but also not to love too deeply. As it is said, 'An affectionate couple cannot grow old together.' My example should serve as a warning to others.

The Time the Spirits Return is, according to custom, the day on which the ghosts of the recently deceased return for a visit to this world. Everything in the house must be arranged the way it was while they were alive, and, particularly, the old clothes they wore must be put on the bed and their old shoes must be put under it, so the ghost can return and see them. Around Soochow, people call this 'the closing of the eyes'. Some would engage a Taoist priest to perform a ceremony in which the spirit would first be called to the bed and then sent away, and this was called 'welcoming the ghost'. The custom in Hanchiang, however, was to set out wine and food in the room of the deceased, after which everyone would leave the house; this was called 'avoiding the ghost'. Some people had even had things stolen while they were out of the house avoiding the ghost.

My landlord was living with me when the time came for Yün's spirit to return, and he left so as to avoid it. Neighbours told me I should set out food and then go away too, but because I was hoping to catch a glimpse of her spirit when it returned, I gave them only vague answers. Chang Yü-men, who was from my home county, warned me about this: 'People have been possessed after toying with the supernatural. You should accept the existence of spirits and not try this.'

'I am staying in the house precisely because I do believe in them,' I said.

'It is dangerous to risk offending a ghost when it returns. Even if your wife's spirit does come home, there will still be a gulf between the dead and the living, so her spirit may not take shape to accept your welcome in any case. All things considered, you should avoid the ghost rather than risk running foul of it.'

I was, however, beside myself with longing for Yün, and paid him no attention. 'It is fate that determines life and death,' I said firmly. 'If you are that concerned about me, why not keep me company?'

'I will stand guard outside the door,' Chang said. 'If you see anything strange, I can come in as soon as you shout.'

I took a lantern and went into the house. I saw to it that everything was arranged the same way as before, but with the sight and sound of Yün gone I could at first not keep myself from weeping sadly. Yet I was afraid that tears would blur my vision and keep me from seeing what I wished to see, so I forced them back, opened my eyes, and sat down on the bed to wait. I touched Yün's old clothes and smelled the fragrance of her that still lingered in them.

It was more than I could bear, and I felt my heart was breaking; stupefied, I began to faint away. But then I thought, how could I suddenly fall asleep while waiting for her spirit?

I opened my eyes, looked all around, and noticed that the glimmering blue flames of the pair of candles on the mat had shrunk to the size of beans. I was frightened, and seized with a cold trembling. Rubbing my hands and forehead, I gazed steadily at the candles; as I watched, both their flames gradually lengthened and grew more than a foot tall, until they scorched the paper pasted over the framework on the ceiling. Just as I was taking advantage of this light to look around, the flames suddenly shrank to their previous size.[35]

By now, my heart was pounding and my knees were trembling, and I wanted to call in my guardian. But then I thought of Yün's gentle and impressionable spirit, and feared she might be repelled by having another man in the room. Instead I just called her name softly and prayed to her, but the room remained silent and there was nothing to be seen. The candle flames then grew bright again, but did not rise up as before. I went out to tell Yü-men what had happened; he thought me very brave, not realizing that in fact I was merely transported with love the whole time.

After I lost Yün, remembering how the poet Lin Ho-ching wrote that 'the plum tree is my wife and the crane my son', I called myself 'he who has lost the plum tree'. For the time being I buried Yün at Chinkuei Hill outside the West Gate at Yangchou, at a place usually called the Precious Pagoda of the Ho Family. I bought a plot for one coffin and left her there temporarily, in accordance with her wishes. Then I took her tablet[36] home, where my mother also grieved for her. Ching-chün and Feng-sen returned home, wept bitterly, and went into mourning with me.

While I was home Chi-tang approached me and said, 'Father is still angry with you, so I think you should go back to Yangchou. After father returns I will explain things and then write and let you know you may come home.'

So I took leave of my mother and said goodbye to my son and daughter, bitterly weeping the while. I returned to Yangchou, where I began to sell paintings for a living. There I often wept at

Yün's grave, utterly alone and in deepest mourning. If I happened to pass by our old house, I found the sight so painful I could hardly bear it. By the time of the Double Ninth Festival, the grass on all the neighbouring graves had turned yellow, while that on Yün's grave alone remained green. The grave-keeper told me hers was a good place for a grave, because the earth spirits there were powerful.

Alone I prayed to Yün saying, 'The autumn wind has grown strong, but I still have only an unlined robe to wear. If you have the power, help me to find work so that I can afford to spend the New Year here while I wait for a letter from home.'

Not long after that, Mr Chang Yü-an, who was a government secretary at Chiangtu,[37] wanted to return to Chekiang for the funeral of one of his parents. He asked me to take his place for three months, and so I was able to buy clothing to keep off the cold. After I left that post, Chang Yü-men invited me to stay with him for a time. He was also unemployed and was having difficulty getting past the New Year.[38] He told me his problems, and I lent him my last twenty golds, telling him, 'This is the money I had put aside for moving my dead wife's coffin home. You must pay me back as soon as I hear from my brother.'

I passed that New Year with Chang. Morning and night I waited, but there was no word from home. Then in the third month of 1804 I received a letter from Ching-chün telling me my father was ill. I wanted to return to Soochow straight away, but was afraid of arousing father's anger again if I did so without permission from him. I was still thinking this over when I received a second letter from Ching-chün with the terrible news that my father had already departed this life. Sorrow cut through me and I called to heaven, but it was too late. With no thought for anything else, I rushed home that night. I beat my head on the ground before father's coffin until it bled, and wailed my grief. Alas! My father had a hard life, always working away from home, and giving birth to an unfilial son like me who seldom gave him happiness and who failed to care for him on his deathbed. How can I avoid punishment for my unfilial crimes?

My mother found me weeping by the coffin; 'Why did you not come home until today?' she asked.

I replied, 'Your son returned only because he was fortunate enough to receive a letter from your granddaughter Ching-chün.' Mother looked at younger brother's wife, then fell silent.

Throughout the seven weeks that I watched over my father's coffin, no one told me anything about the affairs of the household, or discussed with me anything to do with the funeral. For myself, I felt I had failed to behave as a son should, and so did not have the face to ask any questions about these matters.

One day some men suddenly arrived at the house demanding repayment of a loan from me, entering the gate and making a great commotion. I went and heard them out, then said, 'The debts have not been repaid, so you certainly have the right to try to collect them. But my father's flesh and bones are hardly cold. Taking advantage of this misfortune to come shouting your demands is surely going too far.'

Then one of them took me aside and said, 'Someone in your household summoned us to come here and do this. If you will step aside, we will collect the debts from him.'

'I will pay my own debts. You get out of here!' I answered, and they all left meekly.

Because of this incident I called Chi-tang to me and had it out with him. 'Although I, your elder brother, have been unfilial, I have certainly never done anything evil or improper. If you think I have come home just to claim my inheritance, you should know I have not inherited the slightest thing. My hurrying back for the funeral was simply fulfilling my duty as a son. How could you possibly think I wanted to fight about an inheritance? A man's honour lies in being able to stand on his own two feet. I returned with nothing, and I will leave with nothing!' Having spoken I turned and went back to father's coffin, where I lost control of myself and wept loudly.

I then kowtowed in farewell to my mother, and went to tell Ching-chün that I was leaving to search for Chih Sung-tzu deep in the mountains.[39] Just as Ching-chün was trying to talk me out of this, two friends of mine – the brothers Hsia Nan-hsün whose literary name was Tan-an, and Hsia Feng-tai whose literary name was Yi-shan – came looking for me.

They lectured me in strong terms, saying, 'You have every right to be angry with your family for treating you like this. But though your father has died, your mother still lives; and while your wife has passed away, your son is still not established in life. In these circumstances, would your heart really be at ease if you drifted away from the world?'

'Then what would you have me do?' I asked.

'May I humbly offer you lodging in our poor home,' said Tan-an. 'I hear that His Excellency Shih Cho-tang has written saying he is coming home on leave. Why not wait until he returns and then go and pay a call on him? He will certainly have a position to offer you.'

'My hundred days of mourning are not yet completed, and you still have your parents at home. It would just not be right,' I replied.

'Our humble invitation is also our father's wish,' Yi-shan said. 'But if you feel strongly that it would not be right to stay in our home, I am a close friend of the abbot at the Buddhist temple west of there. Why not put up at the temple?' To this I agreed.

Then Ching-chün said, 'Grandfather left not less than three or four thousand golds. You didn't get anything, so how can you not at least take your own travelling bag with you? I'll take it myself to the temple where you will be staying.' And thanks to Ching-chün, in addition to my travelling bag I also ended up with several things my father had left – books, ink stones, and brush holders. The monks at the temple settled me in the Pavilion of Great Mercy. The pavilion faced south, and to its east was a Buddha. I occupied the pavilion's westernmost room, which had a moon window and was directly opposite the shrine, the room where pilgrims would normally have had their vegetarian meals. Near the door there was a very martial-looking statue of Kuan Kung[40] holding a sword.

In the centre of the courtyard there was a ginko tree as big around as the span of three men's arms; its shadow completely covered the pavilion, and in the quiet of the night the wind blowing through its branches sounded like the roaring of an animal. Yi-shan often came to drink with me, bringing wine and fruit, and on one visit he asked me whether I was frightened by the wind at night when I could not sleep.

'All my life I have been honest and free of evil desires,' I replied. 'What have I to be afraid of?'

I had not lived there long before it began to rain heavily, pouring night and day for more than thirty days. At the time I was worried that a branch might break off the ginko tree and smash through the roof, but I relied on the protection of the gods and in the end came to no harm. However, countless walls and houses did collapse in the flood, and the young rice was washed out of all the fields near by. I merely painted with the monks every day, and paid no attention to what was happening outside.

It was the beginning of the seventh month before the weather cleared. Yi-shan's father, whose style[41] was Chun-hsiang, went to Chungming[42] that month on business. I went with him to take care of his books, and got twenty golds for my services. I returned just as my father was to be buried; Chi-tang sent Feng-sen to me to say that 'Uncle does not have enough for the burial, and would like you to help him with ten or twenty golds.' I was going to give him everything I had, but Yi-shan would not allow it, and helped me out by giving half the money. I then took Ching-chün and went first to the grave.[43]

After the funeral I returned to the Pavilion of Great Mercy, until the end of the ninth month when Yi-shan took me with him to collect rent from land he owned at the Yungtai Sands in Tunghai.[44] We spent two months there, and by the time we returned it was already the end of winter. I moved to his home, Snow Goose Cottage, to spend the New Year with him.[45] Though our names were different, he was just like flesh and blood to me.

It was the seventh month of 1805 before Shih Cho-tang returned home from the capital. Cho-tang's real name was Yün-yü, and his literary name was Chih-ju, while Cho-tang was his style. He had been a friend of mine since we were small, and he had taken first place in the Imperial examinations held during the 55th year of the reign of the Emperor Chien Lung.[46] He had been named prefect of Chungking in Szechuan, and was in the field for three years fighting the White Lotus rebels and earning great merit for his actions.[47] We were very glad to see each other when he returned. He was preparing to take his family with him on his return to Chungking to resume office, at about the time of the Double Ninth Festival, and he invited me to go too.

I kowtowed in farewell to my mother at the home of Lu Shang-wu, my ninth sister's[48] husband, because father's old home already belonged to someone else. My mother's parting words to me were: 'Your younger brother is unreliable, so you must work hard on your journey. I look only to you to restore our family's name.' Feng-sen escorted me part of the way but then began to cry, so I told him not to see me off and he turned back.

Cho-tang had an old friend, the second-place degree holder Wang Ti-fu, at the Huaiyang Salt Bureau. When the boat left Chingkou he made a detour to visit Wang and I went along, thus having another chance to visit Yün's grave.[49]

From the time we entered the Yangtze, we enjoyed beautiful scenery all along the route, as the boat worked its way upstream. When we reached Chingchou in Hupei my friend received a letter promoting him to the Inspectorate of the Tungkuan Circuit, so he left me, his son Tun-fu, and all the members of his family at Chingchou temporarily. Cho-tang rode off with only a few things and passed the New Year at Chungking, then went on to his new post from Chengtu via the mountain road.

It was the second month of 1806 before the family continued on by boat to Fancheng, where we all went ashore. The journey then became very difficult, long, and expensive. Horses died and wheels were broken under the weight of the heavy carts loaded with people. We reached Tungkuan at the very beginning of the third month, but by then Cho-tang had again been promoted, this time to be Provincial Judge in Shantso.[50] A light wind could ruffle his sleeves,[51] so his family could not accompany him immediately; he had to ask for temporary lodging for them at the Tungchuan Academy. It was the end of the tenth month before he was paid his salary and allowances from Shantso, and he then sent a man to bring his family to him.

With this messenger he sent a letter to me from Ching-chün with the appalling news that Feng-sen had died young, during the fourth month. I thought back on the tears he had shed when seeing me off, the tears that were an eternal farewell between father and son. Alas!

Yün had only one son, and he did not live to give her descendants. When Cho-tang learned of this he too heaved a deep sigh. He presented me with a concubine, a young woman who renewed in me the spring dreams of life.[52] I was thrown back into the maelstrom of daily existence, a dream from which I do not know when I shall awake.

PART IV

The Delights of Roaming Afar

I have travelled about working in government offices for thirty years now, and the only places in the world I have never been to are Szechuan, Kueichou and Yünnan. The pity is that wheel and hoof have followed one another in such quick succession. Everywhere I have gone I have been accompanying others, so that while beautiful mountains and rivers have passed before my eyes like drifting clouds and I have been able to form some rough idea of what they are like, I have never been able to search out and explore secluded places on my own.

I like to have my own opinion about things and not pay attention to other people's approval or disapproval. In talking about poetry or painting, I am always ready to ignore what others value and to take some interest in what others ignore. And so it is with the beauty of famous scenery, which lies in any case entirely in what one feels about it oneself. Thus there are famous scenic spots which I do not feel are anything extraordinary, and there are unknown places that I think are quite wonderful. This is a record of the places I have visited during my life.

When I was fifteen my father, the Honorable Chia-fu, was employed by County Magistrate Chao at Shanyin.[1] There was then an old scholar in Hangchou, Mr Chao Sheng-tsai, whose real name was Chuan, and County Magistrate Chao invited him to become tutor to his son. My father ordered me to kowtow to him and become his student also.

On days when I had no lessons I would take little trips. One day I went to Ho Mountain, a little more than ten *li* from the city. You could not reach it by land.

Nearing the mountain, you could see a stone cave, with a slab of rock above it that was split in half horizontally and looked as if it was about to collapse. If you rowed your boat in underneath the rock and into the cave, you entered a pool surrounded by high stone cliffs. This was called the Water Garden. By the water's edge someone had built a stone pavilion five spans long. Opposite it the three characters 'admire fish jumping' were inscribed on the stone wall. No one knew how deep the water was, and people said that huge fish lurked on the bottom. I threw out some bait to see what would happen, but only a few small fish rose to it.

Behind the pavilion there was a path to the Land Garden, but that boasted only disorderly piles of small stones made up into an artificial rockery, some of the creations as wide as the palm of a hand, some tall stone pillars with a large rock fixed on top. The chisel marks still remained on all of them, however, and they were not in the least attractive.

Having finished my tour I had something to eat at the Water Pavilion, and told my servant to set off some exploding bamboo.[2] That made a huge noise which all the mountains answered, as if they had heard a clap of thunder. This is how I came to enjoy travelling in my youth. It is a pity that I was not able to visit the Orchid Pavilion or Yü's Tomb,[3] and I regret it to this day.

During the next year at Shanyin my teacher decided he did not want to live so far from his parents because they were growing old, and he moved home. I accompanied him to Hangchou, and thus was able to enjoy visits to the lovely scenery of the West Lake district there. For beauty of design, I think West Lake's Dragon's Well is best, while the Little Paradise Gardens are the next most attractive. Of the mountains in the district, I prefer the Flying Peak of Tienchu and the Auspicious Stone Cave on City God Mountain. I also enjoy the Jade Spring, among the lakes and streams there, because its waters are clear, its fish are abundant, and its liveliness is a delight. Probably the least enjoyable place at West Lake is the Agate Temple at Koling. Similarly, the Pavilion-in-the-Lake and Liuyi Spring: both have their attractions, more than I can describe in fact, but neither can rid itself of the atmosphere of a heavily made-up woman. Neither has the pleasant seclusion of the Cottage of Tranquillity, which is heavenly.

While I was at West Lake, the local people pointed out to me Su

Hsiao's grave beside the Hsiling Bridge.[4] At that time it was covered with only half a mound of yellow earth, but in the 45th year of the reign of the Emperor Chien Lung, his majesty was inspecting the South[5] and asked about it. By the time the great ceremonies were held for his next trip south in the spring of 1784, a stone monument had been put up at her grave, octagonal in shape and with a tombstone mounted on it with the large inscription, 'The Grave of Su Hsiao-hsiao of Chientang'. Since then, poets remembering her have hardly had to wander around searching for her grave.

I cannot help but think of the countless chaste and virtuous women who since ancient days have been buried without being remembered, and of the many who have been remembered for only a short time; yet while this Hsiao-hsiao was nothing but a sing-song girl, everyone since the Southern Chi Dynasty has known of her. Is this because her spirit is supposed to make the lakes and mountains more beautiful?

A few steps north of the bridge was the Chungwen Academy, where I once took examinations with my fellow-student Chao Chi-chih. It was summer then, and the days were long. We rose very early and went out by the Chientang Gate, past the Chaoching Temple, to the Tuan Bridge where we sat on the stone balustrade. The sun was just coming up, and the dawn light behind the willows was most beautiful. A gentle breeze arose, wafting to us the fragrance of the white lotus flowers and refreshing both mind and body. We walked on to the academy, still managing to arrive before the examination questions were issued.

In the afternoon we handed in our papers, and I went with Chi-chih to cool off at Purple Cloud Cave. It was big enough to hold several dozen people, and there was a gap in the rocks at the top that let in a shaft of sunlight. A man had set up some small tables and low chairs to sell wine there, so we loosened our robes and had something to drink, eating delicious dried venison along with fresh water-chestnuts and lotus root. We left the cave slightly drunk.

'Above us is Sunrise Terrace,' said Chi-chih, 'which is very high and has a grand view of the countryside all around. Why don't we take a climb up there?' The idea appealed to me too, and so we bravely climbed up to the peak. From there West Lake looked like a mirror, while the city of Hangchou was as small as a ball and the Chientang River looked like a belt. We could see for hundreds of *li*, quite the most wonderful vista I have ever seen. We sat there a long time, coming down the mountain hand in hand as the sun was setting and the temple bells at South Screen Hill were ringing.

It was a long way to Taokuang and Yünchi, so we did not go. Passing by Hungmenchü we saw there was nothing special about the plum flowers there, nor were we impressed by the ironwood trees at the Kuku Temple. I had thought that Purple Sun Cave would be worth seeing so we looked around and found it, but the mouth of the cave was only the size of a finger and there was nothing there but a little water bubbling out of it. There are tales that tell of a huge cave inside, but unfortunately I was unable to find a way into it.

On the Chingming Festival my teacher went to offer the spring prayers and to sweep his ancestors' graves, and took me along on the trip. The graves were on Tungyo Mountain, at a place in the countryside where there were many bamboo trees. The grave-keeper dug up bamboo shoots which had not yet grown up out of the ground – they looked like pears, only more pointed – and made soup for us. I liked it very much, and ate two bowls.

'Yi!' my teacher said. 'The soup may be good, but it can have a bad effect on the heart and blood. You should eat some meat to offset it.' I had never liked the products of the butcher's shop, however, and so continued eating so many bamboo shoots that I could not finish my rice. On the way back I felt parched, as if my lips and tongue were about to crack.

We passed by the Stone House Cave, but there was nothing much there to see. At the Pleasant Waters Cave the cliffs are covered with wistaria vines. We went inside and found it like a small room, with a bubbling spring from which the water rushed. The pool was only three feet wide and about five inches deep, and while it never overflowed, neither did it ever dry up. I knelt down and took a drink, and it relieved my thirst immediately.

There were two small pavilions outside the cave, and when we sat in them we could hear the sound of the spring. A monk there invited us to see what he called the Ten Thousand-Year Urn. This urn, which was in the kitchen of a near-by Buddhist temple, had a bamboo pipe that led water into it from the spring and kept it full. Over the long years moss about a foot thick had grown up on its sides, and since the water did not freeze in the winter, the urn was not damaged.

During the autumn of 1781, in the eighth month, my father fell sick with malaria and returned home. When he was cold he wanted a fire, and when he was hot he wanted ice. I advised him against this but he did not listen, and so his illness eventually turned into typhoid fever and grew worse daily. I waited on him with soup and medicine, never closing my eyes day or night for almost a month. My wife Yün also became very ill, and was confined to her bed. I felt terrible, there is no way to describe it.

One day my father called me to him and said, 'I am afraid I will not recover. You have studied a few books, but ultimately this will not help you to make a living. I am going to entrust you to my sworn younger brother Chiang Ssu-chi, so that you can continue in my profession.'

When Ssu-chi came the next day I kowtowed to him as my teacher before my father's bed. Not long after that, however, we called in the famous doctor Mr Hsü Kuan-lien to treat my father, and he gradually recovered. Yün also received treatment from Hsü and got better. It was from this time that I began studying to work in government offices. Why record these unhappy events here? I reply, I record them because it was from this time that I abandoned scholarship and began my wanderings.

Mr Ssu-chi's courtesy name was Hsiang. In the winter of that year I went with him to begin studying the work of a government office, in the *yamen* at Fenghsien.[6] There I had a fellow-student whose family name was Ku; his courtesy name was Chin-chien, his literary name was Hung-kan, and his style was Tzu-hsia. He was also from Soochow, and as a person was generous and resolute, honest and not easily swayed by others. He was a year older than I, so I called him elder brother while he invariably called me younger brother; I became very close to him, the first such friend I had ever had. Unfortunately he died at the age of twenty-two, and since then I have been downcast and alone. I am now six and forty years old, adrift in the vast ocean of life. Shall I ever again in this life have a friend as close as Hung-kan? I remember that when I began my friendship with him we were full of the noble thoughts of youth, and we often talked of going to live in the mountains together.

On the Double Ninth Festival that year, Hung-kan and I were both at Soochow. Our elders, Wang Hsiao-hsia and my father, the Honourable Chia-fu, had called in actresses for a performance, and were giving a dinner at our home. I disliked the noise of these affairs, so the day before I had agreed with Hung-kan to climb the heights of Han Mountain,[7] thinking that on the way I could also look for a site to build a house one day.

Yün prepared some wine to take with us, and the next morning Hung-kan came to fetch me as the sun was about to come up. Carrying our wine, we went out of the city by the Hsü Gate and found a noodle shop where we both ate our fill. We crossed the Hsü River and walked to Date Market Bridge in Hengtang where we rented a leaf-boat. It was not yet noon when we arrived at the mountain.

The boatman was a very good fellow, so we told him to buy some rice and cook it for us. The two of us then went ashore and walked first to Chungfeng Temple. This is south of the Chihhsing Monastery and we followed the road to reach it. The temple was hidden deep in the trees. Its gate was peaceful and the monks had little to do, but when they saw we were dressed in ordinary clothes they gave us no particular reception.[8] Our interest was not in the temple in any case, so we did not go in, and by the time we returned to the boat the rice was ready.

When we finished eating, the boatman picked up our wine and came along with us, telling his son to look after the boat. From Han Mountain we went on to the White Cloud Villa at Kaoyi Garden. The balcony there faced a cliff, and below it there had been dug a small pond that was full of clear water and surrounded by stones and trees. Marsh grass and lychee trees hung off the cliff, and the walls of the buildings were covered with moss. We sat beneath the windows and could hear only the rustling of falling leaves. The peace was unbroken by the shadow of any other person.

We told the boatman to sit down and wait for us at a pavilion outside the gate. Entering a fissure in the rocks, a place called a Strip of Heaven, we followed winding steps that led upward to the peak, which was called Above the White Clouds. There was a ruined temple there of which only one of the towers remained standing precariously, but we climbed it and were able to see into the far distance. After resting a while, we came down, holding on to one another.

'When you climbed the mountain,' said the boatman, 'you forgot to take the wine with you!'

'We didn't come on this trip just to climb mountains,' Hung-kan replied. 'We are looking for a place where we could retire.'

'Two or three *li* south of here,' said the boatman, 'is the large village of Shangsha, where there is some vacant land. I have a cousin named Fan who lives in the village. Why don't you go there to have a look?'

'Shangsha was where Mr Hsü Ssu-chai retired at the end of the Ming Dynasty,' I said happily. 'I have heard that his garden is very refined, but I have never been there.'

At this the boatman led us off. The village lay on a road that wound down the valley between two mountains. The garden was on a mountainside and had no rocks in it, but there were many old trees that had grown up twisted and gnarled. The small pavilions and the lattice screens on the windows were all quite simple. It had a bamboo fence and a straw hut, and was just right for the home of someone who had retired. In the middle there stood an acacia tree pavilion; the tree was as big around as the span of two men's arms. Of all the gardens I have seen, this one was the best.

To the left of the garden was a mountain called Chicken Coop Mountain. Its peak rose straight up and on the top there rested a large rock, like the mountain at the Ancient Cave of Precious Stones at Hangchou, though lacking its splendour.

Beside us there was a green rock as big as a bed, and Hung-kan lay down on it, saying, 'From here we can look up and see the mountain peaks, and look down and see the garden. The view is vast and splendid, so let's open the wine!' We persuaded the boatman to drink with us, and were soon singing and whistling to our hearts' content.

The local people knew we had come looking for some land and

mistakenly thought we wanted a grave site, so they told us which places had good *feng-shui*.⁹ 'It doesn't matter where we are buried,' said Hung-kan. 'So long as we like the place, we don't care about its *feng shui*.' (Who could have known that his words would turn out to be a prophecy!)

When the wine jugs were empty, we spent the rest of the afternoon picking wild chrysanthemums to put behind our ears, so that by the time we returned to the boat the sun was about to set. Though it was late when I reached home, the guests from my father's party were still there.

Yün took me aside and said, 'Among the actresses today there is one called Lan-kuan who is quite a lady. You might be interested in her.' On the pretence that my mother wanted to see her, I called her into our room. I took her arm and had a look at her; her figure was full and her skin white.

I looked at Yün. 'She certainly is beautiful. But her name belies her figure.'¹⁰

'Fat people have good fortune,' Yün replied.

'Considering the disaster that befell her at Mawei,' I said, 'where was Yang Kuei-fei's good fortune?'¹¹

Yün then made an excuse to send the girl out, and asked me, 'Did you get very drunk again today?' I told her about all the places we had visited, and she listened enchanted for a long time.

In the spring of 1783 I left Mr Ssu-chi and accepted a position at Weiyang.¹² I was then able to see for the first time the faces of Chin Mountain and Chiao Mountain. Chin Mountain should be viewed from afar, while Chiao Mountain should be seen from close by. It's a shame that while I often travelled back and forth in the vicinity of the two mountains, I never climbed their heights to see the view. When I crossed the Yangtze River heading north to the city, the line of Yü-yang's about 'the green willow walls of Yang-chou' came alive for me.¹³

Pingshan Hall was about three or four *li* from the city, but it was eight or nine *li* by road. Although the scenery along the route was entirely the product of human labour and imagination, it was a natural and idyllic park, and the residence of the Immortals could not have surpassed it.

The loveliest thing about it was that it was actually the gardens of more than ten residences that had all been joined into one, forming a connected whole that stretched away to the mountains. Its principal drawback was its site which, while it was outside the city, still followed the city wall closely for about one *li*. To be truly lovely, a city should sit alone amidst rolling mountains. As it was, building the park so close to the city was quite foolish. Still, while touring its pavilions and its towers, walls and rocks, bamboo and trees, the visitor found that all came into view most naturally, nothing being too conspicuous. If the designer had not had hills and gulleys in his heart, he could never have begun to build such a place.

At the very head of the gardens was Rainbow Park, and after a turn north there was a stone bridge called Rainbow Bridge. I do not know whether the park was named for the bridge or the bridge for the park. When passing by in a boat, people called this place the 'long bank of spring willows'. That this scenery was sited here and not close up to the foot of the city wall is a further illustration of how lovely the design of the park was.

Taking another turn, to the west, you came to a temple on a mound of earth called Little Gold Mountain. With this blocking the view the atmosphere of the place became more tightly compacted, something that is difficult to describe in writing. I was told that the ground there was originally sand and that repeated attempts to build up the mound had failed. The work was finally completed, however, by using several layers of wooden planks to hold the earth in place, a project which cost tens of thousands of golds. Only merchants could have done something like this.

Past this point lay the Shengkai Tower, where the river was comparatively broad and where people came to watch the annual boat races. There the Lotus Flower Bridge spanned the river, south to north. The bridge's gates opened out in eight directions, and on the bridge five towers had been built; Yangchou people called the latter 'four plates and a warm pot'. I thought the bridge looked as if too exhaustive an effort had gone into it, and I did not much care for the result.

South of the bridge was the Lotus Seed Temple, and rising straight up from the middle of the temple was a white Tibetan pagoda. The golden fringes of its roof rose to the clouds, and the red walls of its halls were shaded by pine and cypress. From time to time you could hear the ringing of bells and musical stones[14] from within. No other garden in the world could compare with this one.

Crossing the bridge, you came to a tall three-storeyed tower with painted rafters and flying eaves, colourfully decorated. Beside it there was a mound of stones from Lake Tai, and around it a fence of white stones. The tower was called the Place of Many Clouds, and it was like the centrepiece of an essay. Farther on there was an area known as Shu Hill Sunrise; this was flat and held nothing of special interest, being no more than an addition to the previous scene.

As you approached the 'hill', however, the course of the river gradually narrowed and made four or five bends where the banks had been filled in and planted with bamboo. It was as if that little world was coming to an end, but suddenly a great vista opened before you and the Ten Thousand Pine-Forest of Pingshan lay spread out ahead. The characters 'Pingshan Hall' were written out there by Ou-yang Duke Wen-chung himself.[15]

What people call the Fifth Spring East of the Huai River was there inside a stone cave in an artificial hill. It was no more than an ordinary well, however, the water from which tasted like natural spring water. Another well often taken for the real one is near by – it is in the Lotus Pavilion and is surrounded by a pierced iron railing – but it is artificial and its water is quite tasteless.

The Nine Peaks Garden, located at a quiet spot near the South Gate, is in fact the most naturally charming and, I think, the best of all the gardens in Yangchou. I did not go to Kang Hill, so I do not know what it is like.

All this is just a general description of the gardens. I cannot completely describe all their examples of beauty and skilful workmanship. They probably should be looked upon as a beautiful woman handsomely dressed, rather than regarded as one would a simple country girl. I happened to be visiting just as the grand ceremonies were being held there during the Emperor's inspection tour of the South. All the works had been completed, and the Emperor invited to visit them. Because of this I was able to enjoy a grand spectacle, more magnificent than one can expect to come across in a lifetime.

In the spring of 1784 I accompanied my father when he went to work for County Magistrate Ho at the Wuchiang *yamen*. There his colleagues were the gentlemen Chang Pin-chiang from Shanyin, Chang Ying-mu from Wulin, and Ku Ko-chüan from Tiaohsi. We respectfully prepared a temporary palace when the Emperor visited Nantouyü, and I had my second opportunity to look up to the celestial countenance.

Once, just as night was coming on, I suddenly decided to return home. I took one of the small fast boats used for official business – they fly across Lake Tai with two oars at the side and two sculls at the back, and in Soochow are commonly called 'water-horses' – and arrived at Wumen Bridge in the twinkling of an eye. Riding a crane through the air would not be as exciting as this. I arrived home before dinner was ready.[16]

The people of my county have always liked festivals, but the lavish arrangements that day were even more extravagant than usual. The coloured lanterns were enough to make you dizzy, and the songs and music of the pipes were overwhelming. Things of which the ancients spoke – 'painted pillars and carved beams', 'pearl shades and embroidered curtains', 'jade fences', and 'embroidered doorsteps' – did not surpass our decorations. My friends clamoured for me to help them arrange flowers and put up coloured streamers. When we were free we called everyone together, drank, sang loudly, and gaily strolled about the town. We were young and full of enthusiasm, and nothing tired us out. Even though I was born in peaceful times, I never could have seen such things if I had lived in the countryside.

That year County Magistrate Ho was impeached, so my father accepted an invitation to move to Haining and work there for County Magistrate Wang. There lived there a man from Chiahsing named Liu Hui-chieh, a long-time vegetarian and a superstitious man, who once came to see my father. He lived beside the Tower of Smoke and Rain in a pavilion that faced the river and was called the Home of Water and Moonlight. This was where he chanted sutras, and it was as clean as a monk's cell. The Tower of Smoke and Rain was in the middle of Lake Ching, the banks of which were covered with green willow trees; unfortunately there were not many bamboo trees there. There was a tower, however, from which we could gaze into the distance. The fishing boats spread out beneath it like stars over the little waves, in a scene that was best by moonlight. The monks there made very good vegetarian food.

At Haining my father's colleagues were Shih Hsin-yüeh from Paimen and Yü Wu-chiao from Shanyin. Hsin-yüeh had a son named Chu-heng who was quiet and well bred. We never quarrelled, and he was the second close friend I have had in this life. The pity is that we only met like bits of duckweed drifting on the water, and were not together for long.

While at Haining I once went to visit the Chen family's Garden of Peaceful Waves, which occupied a hundred *mou*[17] of land and which was covered with towers and pavilions, winding lanes and galleries. One pond in the garden was very deep and was crossed by a bridge with six bends in it. In addition, the garden boasted rocks covered with vines that completely hid their chisel marks, and a thousand ancient trees, all of them reaching to heaven. With the birds twittering and the flower petals dropping to the ground, it was like being deep in the mountains. Of all the artificial rock gardens I have seen that were built on flat ground, this one looked the most natural.

Once we gave a dinner at the Cassia Tower there, and you could not smell the food for the scent of the flowers. Only the smell of the pickled ginger was not overcome, but then ginger and cassia both turn more pungent with age, like loyal ministers who are made of strong stuff.

Going out by the South Gate at Haining, you came to the great sea.[18] There were two tides a day, which came rushing across the water like silver dykes ten thousand *chang* long.[19] Boats there could ride these tides, turning with a thrust of the oars to face them when they arrived. Attached to the front of the boat was a wooden plank, formed like a long-handled sword. This cut the water in front of the boat, and as it parted the boat followed the plank into the surging waves of the tide. After a moment the boat would rise from the foam, and if its bow were then turned it would follow along the crest of the wave, covering a hundred *li* in almost no time.[20]

There was a pagoda on the embankment, and on the night of one Mid-Autumn Festival I went there with my father to watch the tide come in. About thirty *li* east along the shore from the pagoda lay Chien Mountain, the peak of which rose straight up and one flank of which stood in the sea. There was a pavilion on the mountain top, with an inscribed plaque that read, 'The Sea is Broad, The Heavens Vast'. The view from the pavilion was boundless, but all that could be seen were angry waves reaching to the horizon.

When my age was five and twenty, I received an invitation to work for County Magistrate Ko at Chihsi in Huichou County.[21] Taking the Chiangshan boat from Wulin,[22] I passed Prosperous Spring Mountain and went ashore at Tzu-ling's Fishing Terrace. The terrace was halfway up the mountain, which itself rose straight up, more than ten *chang*[23] from the water. Can the river at the time of the Han Dynasty really have been level with it?[24] By moonlight we anchored at Chiehkou, where there was an inspection office. The scenery reminded me of the couplet: 'Mountains high and moon small; Rocks rise from the low stream.'[25] Unfortunately I saw only the foot of Yellow Mountain, and did not get a look at the entire face of it.

The town of Chihsi was situated amid ten thousand mountains, a small place full of simple people. Near the town was a mountain called Stone Mirror Mountain. To see the 'mirror', you followed a winding path through the mountains for about a *li* and then came to a cliff with water rushing down its face, and with moist greenery that itself seemed about to begin dripping over the ground. Gradually climbing higher to the middle of the mountain, you arrived at a square stone pavilion with four high walls. The left and right sides of the pavilion were as flat as screens, and the light reflected from their lustrous green surfaces so that you could see yourself in them. It was said that once, if a man looked into them, they would reflect what he had been in a former life. But when Huang Tsao[26] came there, he is supposed to have looked into the walls and seen the image of an ape, and then he set fire to the pavilion and burned the walls so that they lost their powers.

Ten *li* from the town was the Great Cave of Burning Clouds. The rocks there were cracked and interlocked, great slopes twisting in and out, as in paintings by the Woodcutter of Yellow Crane Hill.[27] They were, however, chaotic and lacked order. The rocks of the cave were all of the deepest red. Beside it, there was a small and very peaceful Buddhist temple.

Cheng Hsü-ku, the salt merchant, once invited me to go there, and we had dinner at the place. One of the dishes was meat dumplings, and as a young Buddhist novice stood watching us eat with downcast eyes, I gave him four of them. When we left we wanted to give the monks two coins of barbarian silver as a tip, but the abbot did not know what they were, and would not accept them. I told him that one could be exchanged for over seven hundred cash in green money,[28] but he still refused to accept them, saying there was no place near by where he could exchange them. At that, we got together six hundred cash of water-beetles[29] to give him, which he accepted with thanks.

I went back there with some friends another time, taking along a basket of things to eat. The old monk came up and told me, 'Last time the little disciple did not know what he was eating, and came down with diarrhoea. Please don't give him anything today.' It is apparently sad but true, that a vegetarian stomach cannot stand the taste of meat.

To the friends who were with me that day, I said: 'Men who want to be monks must live in this kind of secluded place, seeing and hearing nothing for their entire lives, so that they can meditate in tranquillity. At a place like Tiger Hill in my home county, all day long there is nothing for the eye to see but bewitching boys and captivating girls, nothing for the ear to hear but the music of strumming instruments and songs, and nothing for the nose to smell but good food and fine wines. How could a monk there make his body like dried wood, or his heart like dead ashes?'[30]

If you went out of Chihsi thirty *li* you came to Jen Village, which every twelve years had a flower and fruit festival in which everyone competed in putting up flower displays. Luckily, I was at Chihsi just at the time of the festival. But though I wanted to go, the town was too poor to have any sedan chairs or horses, so I taught a few people how to cut bamboo to make shoulder poles, and tied a chair between them. Then I hired some men to carry it, and went to the festival that way. Only my colleague Hsü Tse-ting went with me, and people around there who saw us travelling in our sedan chairs could not keep themselves from laughing in surprise.

When we came to Jen Village we found that it had a temple, though I do not know what god they worshipped. In an empty area in front of the temple a tall opera stage had been put up. It had painted beams and squared pillars, all very majestic, but when we looked at them from close up they turned out to be only painted paper wrapped around wood and then varnished over. Suddenly there was the sound of a gong and four men appeared carrying a pair of candles on their shoulders, each candle so big it looked like a broken-off pillar. Then eight men came out carrying a pig as big as a bull that had been raised in common by the villagers for twelve years before being killed as a sacrifice to the god.

Tse-ting laughed. 'The pig had a good long life, but the god's teeth are no less sharp for all that. Still, if I were the god I don't think I would enjoy it.'

'But it all shows the simple, honest faith of the villagers,' I countered.

We went into the temple and found that the pots of flowers and fruits that had been placed in the main worship hall and the courtyard had been selected for their unique natural shapes, instead of having been trimmed and pruned. Most were pines from Yellow Mountain. Shortly afterwards the opera performance began and the people flowed to it like an ocean tide. To avoid the crowd, Tse-ting and I left.

After less than two years at this post I shook my robe in disapproval and went home after having a disagreement with my colleagues. At Chihsi I had seen, in busy offices, behaviour so low and venal I could not bear to witness it, so I left official life and became a merchant. I had a paternal uncle named Yüan Wan-chiu whose business was brewing wine at Hsienjentang in Panchi. Shih Hsin-keng and I invested in the business and became his partners. Yüan's wine was shipped to market by sea, however, and less than a year after we joined the firm Lin Shuang-wen's rebellion broke out in Taiwan, blocking the shipping routes.[31] Our goods piled up, we lost our investment, and I was obliged to return to official work. During the following four years, which I spent at government offices in the Chiangpei region,[32] I did not have one trip enjoyable enough to record.

After that we stayed at the Villa of Serenity for a time, living like Immortals in the midst of life. While we were there, my younger cousin's husband Hsü Hsiu-feng returned from eastern Kwangtung and heard I was not working. 'When all is said and done, you can't for long eat the dew and plough with your brush,' he said kindly. 'Why not go with me to South-of-the-Mountains?[33] You would get more than a fly's head worth of profits out of it.'

Yün encouraged me to go too. 'You should take advantage of this opportunity while our parents are still well and you are still young and strong. Rather than constantly scrimping and saving, it would be better to ensure our happiness at one stroke.'

Having decided to go, I got together some money by borrowing from several friends. Yün herself saw to obtaining embroidered work, as well as items like Soochow wine and crabs steeped in liquor, things that South-of-the-Mountains does not have. After informing my parents, I left with Hsiu-feng on the 10th day of Little Spring.[34]

We went first from Tungpa to the river port at Wuhu.[35] This was my first trip on the Yangtze, and I had a wonderful time. Every night after the boat anchored we would have something to drink in the bow. Once I saw a fisherman with a net not three feet wide, the holes in which, however, were about four inches across. There were iron grommets in each of its four corners, apparently to make it sink more easily.

I laughed and said, 'Granted, the Sage taught us, "Do not use nets with too fine a mesh",[36] but how can the man catch anything with a small net that has holes as big as this one?'

Hsiu-feng explained to me, however, that these nets were specially made for catching the *pien* fish. We watched while the fisherman tied a long rope to the net, then lowered it into the water and raised it quickly several times, as if he were trying to find out whether he had caught anything. Before long, he suddenly pulled the net out of the water with a *pien* fish caught in its mesh.

I could only sigh. 'Evidently my quick glance was not enough to fathom the net's mystery!'

One day we saw a hillock rising straight up from the middle of the river, nothing near it on any side, and Hsiu-feng told me this was Orphan Island.[37] In the island's frosty woods, halls and pavilions rose one behind the other; unfortunately, at the time we had a good wind for passing it, and so could not go ashore for a walk. When we reached Prince Teng's Pavilion,[38] I found that it had been incorrectly described in the unreliable monograph of Wang Tzu-an, like the Tsunching Pavilion of the Prefectural Academy in my Soochow which he wrongly placed by the Main Wharf at Hsü Gate.

Immediately below the pavilion we changed to a boat with a high stern and an upraised bow called a 'sampan', and on it sailed from Kankuan to Nanan[39] where we went ashore. That day happened to be my thirtieth birthday, and Hsiu-feng ordered noodles to wish me long life.[40] The next day we crossed the Tayü Mountains, at the top of which was a pavilion with a tablet that said, 'Look up to the nearby sun', to point out how high it was. The peak of the mountain was split in two, and there was a path through the middle like a stone alley, with cliffs on both sides. Two large stone tablets stood at the entrance to the path. One said, 'Retire from the heights before the rushing torrent', while the other said, 'Having attained your desire, go no further'.[41]

At the peak lay General Mei's Temple; I do not know what dynasty he was from.[42] People talk about plum flowers on the peak there, but I did not find a single tree. Perhaps it took the name Plum Peak from General Mei?[43] Ironically, by the time we reached the place it was almost the month of the winter sacrifice, and the potted plum trees I had brought as gifts had already lost their flowers, while their leaves had turned yellow.[44]

Coming out of the pass through the mountains, I immediately felt aware of a difference in the scenery of rocks and streams.[45] West of the pass there was a splendid mountain, but I have forgotten its name. My sedan-chair bearers told me that there was an Immortal's bed on it, but I hurried past, denying myself the sight in order to complete my journey.

Upon reaching Nanhsiung[46] we rented an old dragon boat.

Crossing Foshan County[47] we saw that on the tops of the walls around their homes, the local people had placed potted flowers, with leaves that looked like wintergreen and blooms that resembled peonies. There were three colours of flower – red, white, and pink – and they were called camellias.

It was the 15th day of the month of the winter sacrifice before we reached the province city.[48] We stayed inside the Chinghai Gate, renting three rooms from a man named Wang in a building that faced the street. Hsiu-feng's goods were all for sale to important officials, so I went with him, visiting customers and making lists. People looking for ceremonial gifts came one after another to purchase our goods, which were entirely sold out within ten days.

Even on New Year's Eve the noise of the mosquitoes was like thunder. When people were going out to congratulate one another on New Year's morning, some wore cotton gowns with only thin silk robes over them. Not only was the weather here different, but the local people, while their physical features were the same as ours, were different in manner.

On the 16th of the first month, three local officials who were friends from my home county took us with them to the river to see the sing-song girls. This was called 'making the rounds on the water', and the girls were called '*laochü*'.[49]

We went out together from Chinghai Gate, took a small boat that looked like half an egg shell with a tent over it, and went first to Shamien.[50] The girls' boats are called 'flower boats'; they were all arranged in two ranks facing one another with a water-lane left between them so that small boats could get through. Each group of some ten or twenty boats was tied to a horizontal timber to protect it from the sea wind. Between each two boats was a wooden stake with a rattan ring around it, and the boats were tied to the ring so they could float up and down with the tide.

The madam of the first boat we called at was called the Lady with the Combed Hair. On her head was a hollow framework of silver wire about four inches high around which she wound her hair, and with a long hairpin she had fixed a flower behind one ear. She wore a short jacket and trousers of black, the trousers reaching to her ankles. A towel of red and green was tied around her waist, and she had taken off her shoes. Her costume made her look like the actors of women's parts in a play.

She bowed and welcomed us to the boat with a smile, and pulled aside the curtain so that we could enter the cabin. Chairs and stools were arranged along each side and in the middle was a large couch. A door led to the stern of the boat.

The woman shouted that guests had arrived, and we immediately heard the sound of shoes pattering out. Some of the girls wore their hair in a bun, some in braids coiled on top of their heads. They had used so much powder they looked whitewashed, and then had used rouge as red as a pomegranate. Some had red jackets and green trousers, others green jackets and red trousers. Still others wore short stockings and embroidered butterfly shoes, or were barefoot and wearing silver anklets. They knelt on the couch or leant against the doorway. Their eyes sparkled, but they said not a word.

I looked at Hsiu-feng. 'What happens now?' I asked.

'After you've had a look,' Hsiu-feng replied, 'call one and she will come to you.' I tried calling one over, and she did come to me happily, giving me a betel nut from her sleeve as a token of respect. I put it in my mouth and took a big bite of it, but it was terribly harsh and I had to spit it out. Wiping my lips on a piece of paper, I found my saliva the colour of blood. Everyone on the boat had a good laugh at me.

Next, we went to the Arsenal, where the girls were dressed in the same fashion. The only difference was that all of them, young and old, could play the mandolin. When I spoke to them, they would only reply, '*Mi?*' ('*Mi*' means 'what'.)[51]

Finally I said, 'People say that young men should not come to Kwangtung, to keep from being led astray by the beautiful girls. But who could be attracted by this gaudy clothing and barbarous southern language?'

'The girls on Chaochou boats dress like goddesses,' said one of my friends. 'We could go and see them if you like.'

Arriving at these boats, we found them lined up like the ones at Shamien. There was a famous madam named Su there, dressed up like a flower-drum lady. The powdered women's[52] clothes worn at her place all had high collars, and the girls wore locks around their necks.[53] Their hair in front came down to their eyebrows, and at the back it reached their shoulders; on top it was drawn up into tufts like the hair of slave girls. Those with bound feet wore skirts, and those without bound feet wore short stockings, butterfly shoes, and long trousers. Since I could only just make out the sounds of their language, and disliked their strange clothing as well, I did not find them very attractive.

Realizing this, Hsiu-feng said to me, 'Across the river from Chinghai Gate there are Yangchou boats, where the girls all dress in the Soochow fashion. If we go there, you're sure to find one you like.'

Another of our friends added: 'What people call the Yangchou boats have only one madam, called Widow Shao; with her there is her daughter-in-law, called Big Sister. They are from Yangchou, but their girls are all from Hunan, Hupei, Kwangtung, and Kiangsi.'

So off we went to the Yangchou fleet, which consisted of not many more than ten boats in two ranks facing each other. The girls on them all wore their hair puffed out on the tops and sides, and used only a little make-up. They dressed in broad sleeves and long skirts, and I could understand them when they talked. The woman called Widow Shao received us attentively.

One of my friends called over another boat, one of the wine boats of which the large ones are called 'constant boats', and the small ones 'sand sister boats'. He wanted to play the host and treat us all, and asked me to choose a girl. I picked a young one whose figure and looks were like my wife Yün's. She had the tiniest feet, and her name was Hsi-erh. Hsiu-feng called out a girl named Tsui-ku. The others each had their own usual girlfriend.

We had the wine boat anchor in the middle of the river and happily drank away until several strokes of the night watch had sounded. By then I had begun to fear I could not control myself and so had firmly resolved to return to our rooms, but my friends told me the city gates had already been locked for the night! This was because the gates of all sea frontier cities are locked as soon as the sun sets, but I had not known this before.

By the time we finished dinner, some of us were lying down

smoking opium while others were hugging the girls and making jokes. The servants then began bringing in quilts and pillows, as if to make a common bed for us all. 'Is there a place to sleep on your main boat?' I quietly asked Hsi-erh.

'There is a *liao* that we could use,' she replied. 'But I don't know ... There might be a guest in it now.' (A *liao* is the top deck on a boat.)

'Let's go and take a look,' I said. I called a skiff and we went over to the Shao boat. Drawing close to it I saw the little fleet's lantern fires facing one another, as if I were looking down a long hallway. As it turned out, the *liao* was empty. The madam welcomed me with a smile, saying, 'I knew there would be an honoured guest tonight, so I made a point of leaving the *liao* open for you.'

'You really are a fairy under a lotus leaf,' I laughed. A servant took a candle and led us to the stern of the boat and up some stairs to a small garret. A long bed occupied one side of the room, and there was a table and some other furniture as well. Lifting up a door-curtain and going further forward, we came to a cabin immediately above the main cabin. The bed was along the side here as well, and in the middle of the wall was a square window inlaid with glass, so that even without candles light filled the room from the lantern of the boat facing ours. The quilts, curtains and dressing table were all very elegant.

'You can see the moon from the balcony,' said Hsi-erh. We opened a window above the door from the stairs and crawled out to the top deck above the stern. A short railing ran around the deck on all three sides. A bright wheel of a moon stood out in the vast sky, and wine boats were scattered over the broad river like aimlessly floating leaves. The lanterns of the wine boats twinkled like the stars spread across the sky. All this plus the small boats shuttling back and forth, and the sounds of music and singing added to the rush of the rising tide, made me feel quite romantic.

'This is the reason why "Young men should not go to Kwang-tung",' I said. 'It's a pity that my wife Yün could not have come here with me.' I turned and looked at Hsi-erh. Under the moonlight she did look a bit like Yün, so I helped her down from the balcony, and we put out the candles and went to bed.

Just before dawn Hsiu-feng and the others came back noisily. I pulled on some clothes and got up to welcome them, but they all scolded me for having run off the night before. 'The only reason was that I was afraid of you pulling off my quilts, or lifting up the curtain to my cabin,' I told them. Then we all went back to our lodgings together.

Several days later I went with Hsiu-feng to the Sea Pearl Temple, which lay in the river and which was surrounded by a wall, like a city. On all four sides, some five feet from the water, were ports where cannon were mounted for defence against pirates; as the tide rose and fell, the gunports alternately seemed to float up out of the water and then to sink back into it, defying the laws of nature.

West of Yulan Gate lay the Thirteen Foreign Firms,[54] the architecture of which looked just like that in a foreign painting. Straight across the river from them was the Flower Ground, Canton's flower market, which had a great many flowers and trees. I had thought there were no flowers I did not know, but here I only recognized six or seven out of every ten. I asked their names and found that some were not even entered in the *Handbook of Collected Fragrances*,[55] though perhaps it was only that I could not understand the pronunciation of their names in the local dialect.

The Sea Screen Temple in Canton was built on a vast scale. Inside the main gate there was a banyan tree as big around as the span of ten men's arms. Its shade was as deep as a canopy's, and its leaves did not fall off in the autumn and winter. The pillars, railings, and window screens of the temple were all made of pear wood. There was a bo tree there, the leaves of which resemble the persimmon. When soaked in water the skin of the leaves could be peeled off, leaving a fine network of veins as delicate as a cicada's wing, which could be bound into small books and used for the copying out of scriptures.

On the way home that day we stopped to see Hsi-erh at the flower boats, and it turned out that neither she nor Tsui-ku had guests. We had tea with them and then were going to leave, but they repeatedly insisted we stay. Before long I felt like going up to the *liao*, but the daughter-in-law, Big Sister, already had a wine-guest up there. I had a word with Madam Shao. 'We could continue our fun with the girls,' I said, 'if they could go back to our rooms with us.'

She agreed, and Hsiu-feng went on ahead to tell the servants to prepare wine and some good food, while I took Tsui-ku and Hsi-erh back to our place. We were all chatting and making jokes when Wang Mou-lau from the sub-prefectural office unexpectedly came by, and we persuaded him to come in and drink with us. As we were about to take our first sip of the wine we suddenly heard confused shouts from downstairs, as if someone there were trying to come up. What had happened was that our landlord had a worthless nephew who, learning that we had brought some girls home, had collected some people to try and blackmail us.

'This is all the result of San-pai's[56] suddenly wanting a good time. I should never have had anything to do with it,' Hsiu-feng angrily said.

'Since things have already come to this,' I replied, 'we should not waste time arguing. How can we get rid of them?'

Mou-lau volunteered to go and have a talk with the men downstairs, and in the meantime I told the servants to go quickly and hire two sedan chairs, intending to see the girls out of the house first, and to think up a plan for getting out of the city later.[57]

It soon became apparent that while Mou-lau was able to keep the men from coming upstairs, he was unable to prevail on them to leave. With the two sedan chairs ready, I ordered my servant, who was very handy with his fists, to go down first and clear a way for us. Hsiu-feng took Tsui-ku and followed him, while I took Hsi-erh and brought up the rear. We rushed downstairs all at once and, with the help of my servant, Hsiu-feng and Tsui-ku escaped by the door. One of the men downstairs grabbed hold of Hsi-erh as we ran past, but I kicked at his arm so that he let go of her. Hsi-erh ran out, with me following behind her. My servant stayed by the door to keep them from chasing after us.

'Have you seen Hsi-erh?' I asked him.

'Tsui-ku has already left in a sedan chair,' he said. 'I saw Hsi-erh come out, but I didn't see her get into one.'

I quickly lit a torch, and in its light saw the empty sedan chair still sitting by the side of the road. I ran to Chinghai Gate and there found Hsiu-feng standing beside Tsui-ku's sedan chair. Again I asked about Hsi-erh. 'She said she would go east, but maybe she ran westwards instead,' he replied.

I turned round and had run back past more than ten houses when I heard someone calling to me from a dark alley. By the light of the torch, I saw that it was Hsi-erh. I put her into the sedan chair and was walking along beside it when Hsiu-feng came running up. 'There is a water-gate we can use to leave the city, at Yulan Gate,' he said. 'I've asked someone to bribe the guard to open it. Tsui-ku has already left, and Hsi-erh should go quickly!'

'You go back to our rooms,' I said, 'and try to get rid of those people. Leave Tsui-ku and Hsi-erh to me.'

We reached the water-gate to find it had already been opened, and that Tsui-ku was waiting for us. I held Hsi-erh with my left hand and pulled Tsui-ku along with my right, and we rushed through the water-gate bowed over and walking like cranes. Just then it began to rain, and the way became as slippery as grease. When we reached the river at Shamien the music and song were everywhere. There were some people in a small boat who knew Tsui-ku, and they called to her to come aboard.

It was then that I noticed Hsi-erh's hair was in disarray, and that her hairpins and earrings were all missing.

'Have you been robbed?' I asked.

'They are my mistress's things,' Hsi-erh said smiling, 'and I've been told they are all pure gold. I took them off as we were coming down the stairs, and hid them in my bag. If they had been stolen, wouldn't you have had to pay for them?'

When I heard her say this, I realized just how good a person she was. I told her to do up her hair and not to tell her mistress anything about what had happened, only to say that there were all kinds of people at our rooms and so we had decided to come back to the boat. Tsui-ku told this to their mistress, adding, 'We are already full of wine and food, but we could eat some rice porridge.'

By this time the wine-guest had left the *liao*, and Madam Shao told Tsui-ku as well as Hsi-erh to accompany me there. I noticed that their embroidered shoes were soaked through with filthy mud. The three of us ate the rice porridge together, satisfying our hunger to some extent.

I trimmed the lamp and we talked on into the night. For the first time I learned that Tsui-ku was from Hunan, and that Hsi-erh had been born in Honan and that her original family name was Ou-Yang. Her father had died, her mother remarried, and she had been sold by an evil uncle.

Tsui-ku then told me of the hardships of their life of constantly welcoming new guests and seeing off old ones. When unhappy they still had to laugh loudly, and when they could not stand the taste of wine they still had to drink a great deal; when sick they still had to entertain guests, and when their throats hurt they still had to sing. There were, she said, rough guests who, if even slightly dissatisfied, would throw wine about, overturn tables, and curse loudly.

These affairs were never investigated by the madam, who on the contrary would say that they had not entertained the guest well enough. She told me too about evil customers who kept up their horseplay from sunset till dawn, until it became unbearable. Hsi-erh was still young and had just come to the boat, so the madam still had some consideration for her, she said. Tsui-ku's tears had been falling unconsciously as she spoke, and now Hsi-erh also began to weep silently. I pulled Hsi-erh to me and held her, comforting her. Tsui-ku I told to sleep in the bed outside, as she was Hsiu-feng's friend.

From then on, they would send someone to fetch me every five or ten days. Sometimes Hsi-erh herself would come to the river bank in a small boat to greet me. Every time I went, Hsiu-feng would come with me; I invited no other guests, and we went to no other boats. One night's entertainment only cost four coins of barbarian silver. Hsiu-feng spent each night with a different girl, which the girls called 'jumping the trough', and sometimes even had two girls at a time. I, on the other hand, stayed only with Hsi-erh.

Sometimes I went alone, and we would have something to drink on the balcony or just talk in the *liao*. I did not order her to sing, and I did not make her drink too much; I was gentle and sympathetic with her. The entire boat was happy about this, and girls from neighbouring boats all envied her. When the girls had free time between guests they would come for a visit if they knew I was in the *liao*, and soon there was not a girl in this group of boats whom

I did not know. Every time I boarded the boat, the girls would call to me without a break. I would look left and right, and have no time to do anything but answer their greetings. You could not have bought this welcome, not for ten thousand golds.

In four months there I spent only a little over a hundred golds and moreover was able to eat lychee and other fresh fruits. It was the happiest time I had ever spent in my life. Later, the madam wanted to sell me Hsi-erh for five hundred golds, but I did not like her pestering me and so made plans to return home. Hsiu-feng had fallen in love, however, so I encouraged him to buy the girl, and returned to Soochow the way we had come.

The next year Hsiu-feng went back there, but as my father refused me permission to accompany him I accepted an offer to work for County Magistrate Yang at Chingpu.[58] When Hsiu-feng came home he told me that because I had not returned to Canton, Hsi-erh had tried to take her life several times. Yi! 'Waking from a half-year's Yang-boat dream, I had a bad name aboard the craft!'[59]

After returning from Kwangtung I worked for the government at Chingpu for two years, during which time I had no enjoyable trips to speak of. Not long after that Yün met Han-yüan, and the family began to boil with criticism of her involvement with a sing-song girl. Yün was so indignant about this that she fell ill, and I set up a shop selling books and paintings with Cheng Mo-an in a side room by our gate, to help pay for some of the medicine she needed.

Two days after that year's Mid-Autumn Festival, Wu Yün-ko, Mao Yi-hsiang, and Wang Hsing-lan invited me to go with them to the Lodge of Repose on West Mountain. At the time, however, I was putting my hand to some calligraphy that needed to be done, and since I had no time to accompany them I told them to go ahead without me.

'If you can manage to get away,' said Wu, 'we will wait for you tomorrow noon at the Temple of the Arriving Cranes by the Shuita Bridge at the foot of the mountains.' I agreed to this, and the next day left Cheng to look after the shop. I walked alone out of the Chang Gate, reached the foot of the mountains and crossed the Shuita Bridge. Then I went west along a path on top of a paddy dyke until I saw a temple facing south with a clear stream running past its gate. I knocked at the door and asked whether this was the Temple of the Arriving Cranes. The fellow who answered the door asked me how I had come, and I told him.

He laughed and said, 'This is the Tehyün Temple. Don't you see the plaque? You have already passed the Arriving Cranes.'

'But from the bridge to here,' I said, 'I didn't see a temple anywhere.'

He pointed back the way I had come. 'See the forest of bamboo inside that earthen wall? That's it.' So I went back, and when I reached the wall found a small gate that was tightly shut. I peered through a crack in the door and saw a low fence and a winding path. Green bamboo grew luxuriant all around, no human voices disturbing its peace. I pounded on the gate, but no one answered.

A passer-by gave me some advice. 'That niche in the wall has a stone in it, that you can use for knocking on the gate,' he said. I knocked experimentally several times and, sure enough, a Buddhist novice came out in answer.

I entered by the path, crossed a small stone bridge and turned west, after which I saw the main gate of the temple. A black lacquered plaque hung above the gate, with the two characters 'Arriving Cranes' written in white upon it. Following them was a long colophon, but I did not have time to look at it carefully. Entering the gate I passed through the Weito Hall,[60] perfectly clean with not a speck of dust anywhere, a room of true serenity. Suddenly I saw another novice coming out of a hallway on the left, carrying a pot. I shouted to him loudly, asking about my friends.

Immediately I heard Hsing-lan laughing in an inner room and saying, 'How about that? I said San-pai would never break his word.'

Then I saw Yün-ko coming out to meet me. 'We kept back breakfast for you,' he said. 'Why have you come so late?' A monk stood behind him, and bowed to me. I asked his name, and he was introduced to me as Monk Chu Yi.

I went into the room and found it was only a small place of three spans, with a panel which read Cassia Pavilion. In the courtyard stood a pair of cassia trees in full bloom. Hsing-lan and Yi-hsiang both stood up and shouted to me, 'You are fined three cups of wine for coming late!'

On the table were both meat and vegetarian dishes, all very fine, and both yellow and white wine. 'How many places have you visited already?' I asked.

'When we arrived yesterday it was already late,' Yün-ko answered, 'and this morning we've only been to Tehyün and Hoting.' Then we sat down and drank happily for some time, and after our meal wandered on from Tehyün and Hoting to eight or nine other places, stopping finally at Hua Mountain. Each spot we visited had its places of beauty, too many to describe fully.

On the summit of Hua Mountain is Lotus Flower Peak, but as it was getting on towards evening we decided to visit it another day. However, the cassia flowers grew in great profusion where we were, so we had an excellent cup of tea under the flowers, then obtained mountain sedan chairs and took the path back to Arriving Cranes.

East of the Cassia Pavilion was the small Pavilion of Approaching Purity, where we found cups and plates already set out for us. Chu Yi was a man of few words, but he loved entertaining and was fond of a drink. We began playing the cassia flower drinking game, continuing until each of us had drunk a round and not ending until the second night watch.

'The moonlight is very lovely tonight,' I said when we finished the game, 'but if we just go to sleep drunk like this, its beauty will be lost on us. Where is there a high place with a good view, where we could go to enjoy the moonlight? That's the only way not to waste this beautiful evening.'

'We could climb up to Flying Crane Pavilion,' suggested Chu Yi.

'Hsing-lan has brought his lute along,' said Yün-ko, 'but we have yet to hear him play. How about him playing for us when we get there?'

We all went together, cloaked in the fragrance of the cassia flowers along a road bordered by a frosty forest. The sky stretched out empty and vast in the moonlight, and all the world was silent. At the pavilion Hsing-lan played 'Three Variations on the Plum Blossom' on his lute,[61] and we felt as if we were floating off to the land of the Immortals. Caught up in the spirit of the moment, Yi-hsiang pulled an iron flute out of his sleeve and began playing a plaintive tune on it.

'Even the people watching the moon on Stone Lake tonight cannot be as happy as we are,' said Yün-ko. This was a reference to the festivities for watching the reflections of the moon in the ripples on the water beneath Hsingchün Bridge, which were held each year on Stone Lake in my Soochow on the 18th day of the eighth month. The excursion boats were always packed in rows and the music and singing went on from sunset to dawn. While this was called watching the moon, however, in fact it amounted to nothing more than playing around with sing-song girls and noisy drinking. Before long the moon went down and a cold frost set in, so we returned to the temple and slept, happy and tired.

The next morning, Yün-ko addressed us all: 'There is a temple called Wuyin around here, that is supposed to be most wonderfully secluded. Have any of you ever been there?' We told him that far from having been there, none of us had ever even heard of it.

'Wuyin Temple has mountains on all four sides, and is so out of the way that even monks cannot bear it for long,' Chu Yi said. 'I went there once some time ago, but it had already fallen into ruins. I haven't gone back since it was restored by Retired Scholar Peng Chih-mu. I might still recognize it, though, and if you would like to go there I would be happy to be your guide.'

'Are we supposed to go on an empty stomach, then?' asked Yi-hsiang.

'I have already had vegetarian noodles prepared,' Chu Yi said laughing, 'and we can get a monk to carry a wine basket along for us.'

After we finished the noodles, we set out on foot. As we were passing the Kaoyi Garden, Yün-ko said he wanted to visit the White Cloud Villa there. We went in and sat down, and a monk gravely walked out towards us. He folded his hands, bowed to Yün-ko, and said, 'I haven't seen you for two months. What news is there in the city? Is the provincial governor still in his *yamen*?'

Yi-hsiang jumped to his feet. 'Baldy!' he shouted.[62] He shook his sleeves in anger and stalked off. Stifling our laughter, Hsing-lan and

I left with him. Yün-ko and Chu Yi exchanged a few words with the monk out of politeness, then also took their leave.

Kaoyi Garden was the grave of the honourable Fan Wen-cheng,[63] and the White Cloud Villa was just beside it. The villa had a balcony that faced a cliff overhung with wistaria vines. Beneath this a pond had been dug, about a *chang*[64] across, filled with clear water; there were goldfish swimming around in it, and it was called the Alms Bowl Spring. Near by was a bamboo stove for making tea, placed very nicely. Behind the balcony we could see the general outlines of the Fan Garden, amidst a profusion of greenery. It was a pity that monk was so vulgar, and that because of him we did not feel like staying longer.

By this time we had gone from Shangsha Village past Chicken Coop Mountain, the same place where Hung-kan and I had climbed the heights.[65] The scenery was the same, but Hung-kan was dead, and I was overcome by thoughts of how life passes by. As I walked along dispiritedly we suddenly came to a stream blocking the road, and could go no further. There were a few village boys there picking mushrooms in the wild grass, who poked out their heads and laughed at us as if they were surprised to see so many people come by. We asked them how to get to the Wuyin Temple, and the reply was, 'The road ahead is flooded, so you cannot go that way. Be good enough to go back a short distance to the south where there is a small path. Take it over the mountain and you'll be there.'

We did as they said, crossed the mountain and walked south for several *li*, but gradually found ourselves in a wilderness of bamboo and trees, surrounded by mountains. By now the path itself was covered with green moss, and there was not a sign of humanity. Chu Yi looked around doubtfully, and said, 'It seems to me as if it should be here, but this path is not taking us anywhere. What do we do now?'

I squatted down and looked around carefully. Hidden behind a thousand bamboo trunks I saw a jumble of rocks, walls, and buildings. Pushing our way through the dense bamboo we went over to have a look, and finally came to a gate above which was a panel reading 'Wuyin Temple, restored by the Old Man of the

South Garden, one Peng, in such-and-such a year, month, and day'. Everyone was delighted, and said, 'If it hadn't been for you, this temple would have been like the spring at Wuling.'[66]

The temple gate was tightly closed, and though we knocked for some time there was no answer. Suddenly a side door opened with a creaking sound, and a young man in ragged clothes stepped out. His complexion was sickly, and his shoes were falling apart. 'What do you want?' he asked.

Chu Yi bowed his head and replied, 'We admire the serenity of this temple, and have come specially to pay our respects.'

'This is a poor temple. The monks have gone and there is no one to receive you. You ought to find another place to visit.' When the young man had finished speaking he made as if to go inside and shut the door, but Yün-ko quickly stopped him and promised him a tip if he would open the gate and let us look around.

'It's just that there isn't even any tea,' said the young man, smiling now, 'and I was afraid of being rude to you. How could I have been thinking about a tip?'

As soon as he opened the temple gate we saw the face of the Buddha, its golden reflection mingling with the green shade. The steps of the hall and the stone foundations were covered with moss as delicate as embroidery. Behind the hall, steps rose like a wall and led to a terrace with a stone balustrade round it. Following the terrace to the west we came upon a rock shaped like a loaf of steamed bread. It was about two *chang*[67] high, and its base was surrounded by small bamboo trees.

Going further west and then turning north, we climbed the rock by going up the steps of an inclined verandah. Immediately opposite the large rock was a guest house of three pillars. Beside it a small moon pool had been dug; it was fed by a clear spring and criss-crossed with watercress. East of the guest house was the main hall. To the left of the hall and facing west were the monks' quarters and the kitchen; behind it was a cliff, and there you could not see the sky for the deep shade of many trees. Hsing-lan and I were exhausted by this time, and took a little rest beside the pool.

Just as we were about to open the wine basket and have a drink, we suddenly heard Yi-hsiang's voice from the tree-tops: 'San-pai, come quickly! There is a beautiful view here.' We looked up but could not see him, so Hsing-lan and I followed the sound of his voice. We went out by a small door in the eastern side room of the hall and turned north, where we went up dozens of stone steps, just like a ladder. Then, ahead of us, we made out a building in a bamboo grove. Climbing the steps of the building, we found that on the top floor it had eight windows giving a clear view all around, and a plaque reading 'Flying Cloud Pavilion'. Mountains spread around on all sides like a wall, except for the south-west where we could see the water washing the sky in the far distance. Tiny sails blew in the wind there, on what was Lake Tai. Looking down from the windows we saw the wind blowing the tops of the bamboo into waves, as if it were a wheat field.

'What do you think?' Yi-hsiang asked me.

'It really is very lovely.'

Then we heard Yün-ko calling from west of the tower, 'Yi-hsiang, come quickly! It is even more beautiful here.' We climbed down again, and walked about a dozen paces west, where the ground cleared into an open plateau, like a terrace, which we guessed must have been at the top of the cliff that rose behind the temple hall. Broken bricks and parts of a foundation still remained there, apparently the ruins of an earlier temple. All around were the surrounding mountains, and the view was even grander than that from the pavilion. Yi-hsiang gave a long shout in the direction of Lake Tai, and all the mountains echoed it. We sat down on the ground, opened the wine jar, and suddenly felt hungry. The young man from the temple offered to make us tea from some scorched rice, but we told him to make rice porridge out of it instead.

We invited him to eat with us, and asked him why the temple had fallen into such disrepair. 'There are no neighbours around here, and at night there are many robbers,' he said. 'Whenever we have something to eat they come and steal it. As for the vegetables and fruits that we plant, half of them end up with the wood-cutters. This place is under the jurisdiction of the Chungning Temple, but every month they send us only a stone[68] of dried rice and a pot of salted vegetables. I'm living here for a while to look after the temple for

Peng's descendants, but I'll be leaving soon and there will be no trace of anyone here then.'

Yün-ko gave him a coin of barbarian silver in thanks, after which we returned to Arriving Cranes, rented a boat, and went home. Later I did a picture called 'Painting of Wuyin', and gave it to Chu Yi in memory of our delightful trip.

In the winter of that year I acted as the guarantor for a friend's loan, lost favour with my parents, and so went to stay with the Huas at Hsishan. The next spring I wanted to go to Weiyang,[69] but was short of money. My old friend Han Chun-chuan was then working in the magistrate's office at Shangyang,[70] however, so I went to visit him to see if he could help me. My clothes were old and my shoes were worn, so I did not dare to go into his office; instead, I sent him a note asking him to meet me in the park at the county temple. When he came and saw me he realized what a sad state I was in, and helped me out with ten golds. The park there was built with a grant from a merchant who traded abroad, but while it was very large its layout, unfortunately, was disorderly, and its artificial stone mountains did not show any sense of arrangement.

On my way back I suddenly recalled the beauty of Yü Mountain, and fortunately there was a boat going conveniently near there.[71] The time was the second month of spring, and the peach and plum were in full bloom. The only unpleasant thing about the journey was that I had no one to keep me company.

Carrying three hundred copper cash, I casually strolled to Yü Mountain Academy. Looking up from outside its wall I saw a mass of trees filled with flowers, all of delicate reds and fresh greens. The academy lay by a stream and close to some mountains, and was very lovely. Unfortunately I was unable to find its gate, however, and so simply asked a passer-by what road I should take to go on to Yü Mountain. Soon I came to a tea-seller's mat shed and went in for a cup of *pilochun*,[72] which was delicious. I asked a traveller there where was the best scenery on Yü Mountain; 'Go through the Western Pass, and near Sword Gate you will find the most beautiful spot. If you want to go, though, please let me be your guide.' I went with him, happy to have his advice.

Taking the Western Pass, we followed the foot of the mountain through several *li* of hilly country until we gradually saw the mountain peak rising before us, its rocks in distinct horizontal layers. We could see when we reached it that the mountain was split into two cliffs, one concave and one convex, several tens of *jen*[73] high. As I gazed upwards from close by it seemed as if the mountain was about to collapse on me. 'People around here say there's a cave up there that gives a view as beautiful as any in the land of the Immortals. It's a pity there's no road up,' said my companion.

This only served to rouse my interest and, rolling up my sleeves and tying up my robe, I climbed like an ape straight up to the top. The so-called cave was only about one *chang*[74] deep, and there was a crack in the rock at the top through which I could clearly see the sky. Looking down I felt my legs weaken as if I were about to fall, so I descended with my stomach to the cliff, clinging to the vines. My companion sighed and said, 'Good man! I have seen brave travellers before, but never one like you.'

I was thirsty and wanted a drink, so I invited him to a rough shop where I bought us three cups of wine. As it was getting dark and the sun was about to set, I did not make a complete tour but returned to where I had been staying with a dozen pebbles of iron ore that I had picked up.[75] I shouldered my satchel and took a night boat to Soochow, returning to Hsishan from there. This was a delightful trip that I took in difficult times.

The tragedy of my father's death occurred in the spring of the 8th year of the reign of the Emperor Chia Ching; I was about to leave home and become a recluse when my friend Hsia Yi-shan insisted that I stay a while at his home. That autumn, during the eighth month, he invited me to go with him to Yungtai Sands at Tunghai where he was going to collect his share of some crops. The Sands lay in Chungming County over a hundred *li* by sea beyond Liuhokou.[76] They had newly risen from the water and had just been brought under cultivation, being still covered with reeds and with no streets or markets and very few other signs of habitation. There was only a granary of several dozen spans owned by a man named Ting who was in the same business as Yi-shan. A moat had been dug around his granary on all four sides, and outside that a surrounding embankment had been raised and planted with willows.

Ting's literary name was Shih-chu. He came from Chungming, and was the leading settler on the Sands. His accountant was named Wang, and they were both lively and amusing men, fond of guests and not concerned about standing on ceremony. As soon as we met, it was as if we were old friends. If we wanted to eat, Ting would kill a pig, and if we felt like drinking he would overturn the wine jar. When we were drinking he would play only finger games because he knew nothing of literature, and when we were singing he would only shout because he could not carry a tune. After he had been drinking, he would order his workers to stage fights to entertain us.

Ting kept over a hundred head of cattle, which were allowed to roam free on the embankment, and he also kept geese to give an alarm against pirates. In the daytime he would go hunting among the reeds and dunes with a falcon and a dog, and would bag many a flying bird. I sometimes went on the chase with him, lying down to sleep wherever we happened to be if I grew tired.

Once Ting took me to the fields where the crops were ripe. Each field had a number and was surrounded by a high embankment to protect it from the tides. The dykes all had sluices that could be opened or shut with gates. If the fields were dry the gates could be opened at high tide to irrigate them, and when they were flooded the gates could be raised at low tide to drain them.

The field hands lived spread out like stars in the sky, but could be assembled at a shout. They addressed the owner as 'landlord', and were obedient, sincere, and pleasant. If angered by unfair treatment they became wilder than wolves or tigers, but if spoken to pleasantly as equals they quickly turned submissive. They lived according to the wind and the rain, the dark and the light, as men did in greatest antiquity.

Looking out from my bed there I could see the rolling breakers, and from my pillow the tides sounded like the beatings of the gongs and drums of war. One night I saw a red light as big as a willow basket floating at sea several dozens of *li* away, and then saw the sky light up with red rays as if from a great fire. 'When spirit lights and spirit fires appear here it means that more sands will rise from the water before long,' Shih-chu told me later.

Yi-shan was always happy and fun-loving, but here he let himself go even more. I became less inhibited myself, singing crazily from the back of a buffalo or dancing drunkenly on the beach. I did whatever my heart desired, and this was the most relaxed and happiest trip of my life. We did not complete our business and return home until the tenth month.

Of the beautiful scenery at Tiger Hill in my Soochow,[77] I prefer a site behind the mountain called A Thousand Clouds; next to that, I enjoy the Sword Pool most.[78] Most of the other scenic spots there are obviously man-made and are spoiled by decoration so that they have lost the true look of mountains and forests. As for the newly built Temple to the Honourable Pai and Pagoda-Shadow Bridge, they are only so many pleasant-sounding names from the past. The Yehfangpin, the name of which I once rewrote with different but similar-sounding characters for the fun of it, is even more crowded with decoration which only makes it look like a woman too heavily made-up.

The most famous place in Soochow itself, Lion Forest,[79] was supposedly created in the style of paintings by Yün-lin with splendid rocks and many old trees,[80] but to me it looks more like a pile of coal dust covered with moss and ant hills, without the least suggestion of the atmosphere of mountains and forests. In my humble opinion there is nothing particularly wonderful about it.

Lingyen Mountain was the ancient site of the King of Wu's Kuanwa Palace.[81] On the mountain lie Hsi-shih's Cave, the Walk of Musical Shoes, and the Canal Where Perfumes are Gathered. All of them, however, are laid out carelessly, merely spread out without any organization, and lack the great beauty of the Tienping and Chihhsing Hills.[82]

Another name for Tengwei Mountain was Yüan's Tomb. It backed up on to Lake Tai to the west and faced Chin Peak to the east, its red cliffs and green pavilions making it look like a painting. The people who lived there planted plum trees for a living, and when the flowers bloomed all you could see for dozens of li appeared to be a heavy fall of snow; for this reason the area was called the Sea of Fragrant Snow.

To the left of the mountain there were four ancient cypress trees that people called by the names 'Pure', 'Rare', 'Ancient', and 'Strange'. 'Pure' had a straight trunk flourishing into green branches. 'Rare' sprawled on the ground, and had three twists in its trunk. 'Ancient' had bald branches at the top, and was flat, broad, and half decayed, so that it looked like the palm of a hand. The trunk of 'Strange' spiralled up like a conch shell, and its branches did the same. It was said that these trees dated from before the Han Dynasty.

In the first month of 1805 Yi-shan's respected father Mr Chun-hsiang and his uncle Chieh-shih led four of their sons and nephews to Pu Mountain to perform the spring sacrifices at the family temple and sweep the ancestors' graves; they invited me to accompany them. We proceeded first to Lingyen Mountain, then crossed Tiger Mountain Bridge, and from the Feichia River entered the Sea of Fragrant Snow to see the plum flowers. Their temple on Pu Mountain was covered by, indeed, was hidden in, this Sea of Fragrant Snow. The plum flowers were in full bloom at the time, and even our coughing and spitting were perfumed by them. I later painted a set of twelve pictures titled 'Paintings of the Scenery and Woods of Pu Mountain', and presented them to Chieh-shih.

In the ninth month of that year I accompanied His Excellency Shih Cho-tang when he went to take up his duties as magistrate of Chungking in Szechuan. Going up the Yangtze our boat stopped at Huancheng;[83] at the foot of near-by Huan Mountain lies the tomb of the Honourable Yü, a loyal minister during the closing years of the Yüan Dynasty.

Beside the tomb is a hall of three spans called the Grand View Pavilion, which faces South Lake and has its rear wall towards Chien Mountain. The pavilion is on the ridge of a hill, and from there we could see a great distance. A long verandah stretched along its side, the windows opening to the north. At the time, the leaves were just beginning to turn red with the frost and were as bright as peach or pear leaves.

My travelling companions were Chiang Shou-peng and Tsai Tzu-chin. South of the Huancheng city wall lay Wang's Garden. The piece of ground on which it stood was broad from east to west, but narrow from south to north, because on the north it backed up directly on the city wall, while to the south it abutted on to the lake. This limited area presented many problems of design which I found had been solved by building the garden according to the methods of doubled terraces and storeyed halls.

By doubled terraces I mean that the terraces on the tops of the buildings were extended into hanging roof gardens, and rocks arranged and flowers planted up there so that a visitor would never know that a building lay beneath his feet. The rocks were arranged on top of the buildings while the gardens were placed on the overhanging portions, so that the flowers and trees could grow nurtured by the influence of the earth below.

By storeyed halls I mean that above the buildings were built balconies, and above the balconies were built terraces, the whole consisting of four storeys stepping up from one to the next. These even had small ponds where the water was retained, and the design was such that a visitor could hardly tell what was illusion and what was reality.

The foundations of these buildings were all made of brick and stone, with the places needing heavy support using pillars made in the Western fashion. Fortunately the buildings faced South Lake, so there was no obstruction of the view. I strolled through the garden elated, finding it better than gardens built on flat ground and a wonder of workmanship.

The Yellow Crane Pavilion at Wuchang[84] lies on Yellow Goose Point, which, back from the shore, rises to become Yellow Goose Mountain, usually called Snake Mountain. The pavilion is three storeys tall, with painted beams and flying eaves, and stands on a peak beside the city facing the Han River and just opposite the Chingchuan Pavilion at Hanyang.

While we were there, Cho-tang and I braved the snow to climb up to it. The empty sky stretching above, the hortensia flowers dancing in the wind, and the silver mountains and jade trees in the distance, made me feel as if I were on a jasper terrace of the Immortals. Little boats sailing back and forth on the river were being tossed in all directions, like fallen leaves thrown about by the waves. Dreams of worldly fame and fortune faded before such a scene. There were a great many poems written on the walls of the pavilion. I cannot recall them all, but I do remember one that was written on two columns:

> When will yellow cranes come again,
> and we empty our gold cups
> over old flowers on the islands?
>
> Now the clouds are flying past me,
> and who will play the jade flutes
> over May plums by city and stream?

The Red Cliffs of Huangchou are outside the Han River Gate of the prefectural capital.[85] The cliffs rise from the banks of the river that separates them, and are all a deep red colour, hence their name. The Waterways Classic[86] calls them Red Nose Mountain. Su Tung-po came here and wrote two poems in the *fu* style, in which he erroneously said the place was the site of a battle between the forces of Wu and Wei.[87] The water has now receded from the base of the cliffs, but on the top of them there remains the Pavilion of the Two *Fu* Poems.

In the second month of winter that year we reached Chingchou. There Cho-tang received the letter promoting him to the Inspectorate of the Tungkuan Circuit, and left me behind at Chingchou. I was disappointed at being denied this opportunity to see the mountains and rivers of Szechuan.

On his departure for Szechuan, Cho-tang also left behind at Chingchou his son Tun-fu, his family, Tsai Tzu-chin, and Hsi Chih-tang. We stayed at the remains of the Liu Family Garden, and I remember there was a plaque above the garden's main hall that read, 'Mountain Home of Wistaria and Red-trees'. The halls were all encircled by stone balustrades. In the middle of a square pond one *mou*[88] in size a pavilion had been built with a stone bridge leading to it. The area behind the pavilion had been landscaped with earth and rocks, and was covered by a profusion of trees. Apart from this, however, there was a lot of empty ground, because the remaining towers and pavilions all lay in ruins.

None of us had anything to do, and so we whistled and sang, took walks, or gathered together to chat. By the end of the year we had had to cut down on our spending, but everyone was quite pleasant about it. We pawned some of our clothes to buy wine, and even bought gongs and drums to beat at New Year. Every night we drank, and every time we drank we played drinking games. We were so poor that four ounces of strong liquor became a great feast.

One day we met a man named Tsai from our home county; when Tsai Tzu-chin and he talked over their ancestry it turned out that they were distantly related, Tzu-chin being of the junior branch of the family. We asked this Tsai to take us to some famous scenic spots in the area, and the first one he chose was Winding River Tower in front of the Prefectural Academy. While Chang Chiu-ling was prefectural magistrate here he wrote poetry on top of the tower.[89] Chu Hsi[90] also wrote a couplet about the place:

> In longing, I can only
> climb Winding River Tower.

Above the town there is the Hsiungchu Tower, built by Kao during the Five Dynasties time. It is on a huge scale, and by looking hard you can see for a distance of several hundred *li* from the top of it. Weeping willows were planted all along the rivers which surrounded the town, and with the little boats being rowed back and forth across them, the rivers looked just like paintings.

The Chingchou prefectural offices had been the headquarters of the Faithful and Loyal Duke Kuan;[91] inside the gate to the private quarters there was a damaged granite horse-trough that was supposed to have been where Red Hare Horse fed.[92] We wanted to visit Lo Han's house on a small lake west of the city, but could not find it. We also wanted to visit Sung Yü's old home north of the city. Once Yü Hsin had stayed there while fleeing to Chiangling during Hou Ching's rebellion.[93] It was supposed to have been turned into a wine house, but we could not find it.

It snowed on New Year's Eve that year, and afterwards turned very cold. On the first day of the year we did not have to bother making New Year calls,[94] and so spent the day with only the lighting of firecrackers, the flying of kites, and the making of paper lanterns to entertain ourselves.

Soon the rain washed the spring earth and the wind brought a message of growing flowers. Cho-tang's concubines brought his young daughters and sons down river, Tun-fu reorganized the baggage, and all of us set off together. We landed at Fancheng and went directly to Tungkuan.

From the west of Wenhsiang District in Honan we entered Hanku Pass. There is an inscription of four characters there that says, 'A Purple Mist Comes from the East', in memory of the time Lao-tzu passed that way riding a black water buffalo.[95] The pass was a defile between two mountains that allowed only two horses to pass at the same time.

After about ten *li* we arrived at Tungkuan, which has a steep cliff behind it on the left and on the right faces the Yellow River. The passage lay between the mountain and the river, and directly blocking it was an imposing fort of many towers and battlements. Its carts and horses were silent, however, and there were few signs of habitation. Describing the desolation of the place, Chang Li wrote, 'The sun bakes Tungkuan's four open gates.'[96]

The Inspectorate had only an assistant sub-prefect under it. The offices were next to the north wall of the city, and had a vegetable garden of some three *mou*[97] behind them extending along the wall.

Two ponds had been dug near the offices, one on the east side and one on the west, and a stream brought in from outside the south-west wall. It flowed east to a point between the two ponds and then divided into three courses: one flowed south to the main kitchens and supplied all daily needs, one flowed on east into the eastern pond, and one flowed north and then west and spurted into the western pond from the mouth of a stone dragon. The water drained from this pond via a sluice in its north-west corner, then ran north by the base of the city wall and out through a drain straight down to the Yellow River. Day and night, the sound of the encircling water fell on our ears with extraordinary clarity. The shade of bamboo and trees was so thick you could not see the sky.

In the centre of the western pond there was a pavilion surrounded by lotus flowers. East of it was a library of three rooms that faced south; it had a vine arbour in the courtyard where there was a square stone table for playing *wei-chi*,[98] or for having a cup of wine. The rest of the grounds were all planted with chrysanthemum beds. To the west of the pavilion was an open hall of three rooms which faced east and from which you could hear the sound of the flowing water. At the south end of the hall was a small door to the inner apartments, and at the north end were windows over-looking another small pond. North of that pond was a small temple for the worship of the Flower Goddess. The centrepiece of the garden was a building three storeys tall close up to the north city wall. Looking over the wall from there you could see the Yellow River and, north of the river, mountains stretching out like a screen. They lay in Shansi Province, and were a truly magnificent sight.

I lived in the south of the garden, in a house shaped like a boat. On top of a hill in the courtyard stood a small pavilion where you could get a general view of the centre of the garden. It was shaded on all sides and cool in the summer. For me, Cho-tang named my house the Unmoored Boat,[99] and this was the loveliest house I ever had during all my official travels. Near the hill on which it stood several scores of different varieties of chrysanthemum were artfully laid out, but unfortunately Cho-tang was transferred to the position of Provincial Judge in Shantso before the flowers even began to bud.

The family then moved to the Tungchuan Academy, and I moved along with them. Cho-tang went ahead to take up his duties in Shantso. Tzu-chin, Chih-tang and I were like the rest of the staff in having nothing to do in Cho-tang's absence, and so we often went out on little trips.

Once we took sedan chairs and horses and went to the Huayin Temple, passing through Huafeng Village where Yao[100] prayed three times. Inside the temple grounds were many Chin Dynasty locust trees and Han Dynasty cypress trees, most as big around as the span of three or four men's arms. Cypress trees there had grown up surrounded by locust trees, and locust trees had grown up surrounded by cypresses. The halls of the temple had many ancient stone tablets, one inside being an inscription by Chen Hsi-yi of the characters 'good fortune' and 'long life'.

At the foot of the Hua Mountains was the Jade Spring Monas-tery, where Mr Hsi-yi shed his earthly form and became an Immortal. On a stone bed in a cave the size of an attic there was a clay figure of him sleeping. The near-by countryside had fresh water and brilliant sand, and many plants of a deep red colour. The spring-fed stream for which the monastery was named flowed very quickly, and the whole area was thick with tall bamboo. Outside the cave was a square pavilion with a plaque reading 'Carefree Pavilion', and beside it were three ancient trees cracked like split coal, and with leaves that resembled those of the locust tree, only of a deeper colour. I do not know their name, but the local people called them 'carefree trees'.

I do not know how many thousands of *jen*[101] high the Hua Mountains are. Unfortunately I could not pack up some food and go to climb them.

On the way back from the Huayin Temple I saw some persimmons that had just ripened growing in the forest, and picked some from horseback to eat them. The local people shouted to me to stop, but I did not listen and bit into one. It was terribly bitter and I spat it out immediately. I got off my horse looking for a spring, and couldn't talk until I had rinsed out my mouth, a sight at which the local people laughed loudly. After the persimmon is picked it has to be boiled for a while before it loses its bitterness, but I had not known this.

At the beginning of the tenth month Cho-tang sent a man from Shantung to fetch his family, and we left Tungkuan and went from Honan to Shantung. In the western part of Chinan city in Shantung lies Lake Taming, in the centre of which are the beautiful Lihsia Pavilion and the Fragrant Water Pavilion. It must have been lovely in summer to take some wine and drift in a boat there, in the deep willow shade amidst the fragrance of the lotus flowers. It was winter when I went there, however, and all I saw were bare willows and cold mists rising from the vast expanse of water.

Paotu Spring is the crowning glory of Chinan's seventy-two springs. It is split into three pools and from under the ground water rushes up fiercely, as if it were boiling. Another strange thing about it is that while the water in all other springs flows down from above, its water flows up from below. Beside the spring is a building dedicated to the worship of Ancestor Lü, the patron of medicine, and many travellers stop here for a sip of tea.

In the second month of the next year I took an appointment at Laiyang. In the autumn of 1807 Cho-tang was dismissed from office and appointed to the Hanlin Academy, and I accompanied him to the capital. I never got to see the so-called mirage of Tengchou after all.

This is the end of Six Records of a Floating Life, *as we have it. Virtually nothing is known of Shen Fu's life after the conclusion of this chapter.*

Appendices

1 A History of Life at Chungshan

As was mentioned in the Introduction, this chapter and the one
following were supposedly rediscovered in the mid-1930s, when
they were published by the World Book Company of Shanghai,
which released what was claimed to be the first complete edition
of the *Six Records*. Close readers of the original four-chapter
edition, however, almost immediately spotted them as fabrications.*

Their first clue came in the first four characters of this chapter,
which date its events – purportedly an account of a journey Shen
Fu made to the Ryukyu Islands – as occurring in 1800. As those who
have glanced over our chronology will note, however, Shen Fu was
a very busy man that year, and nowhere makes reference to leaving
the country.

In fact, much of this 'chapter' is copied – cleverly, but in many
places word for word – from *Record of a Mission to the Ryukyu
Islands* by Li Ting-yüan. Li, a well known scholar of his day, wrote
the book after having been sent by the Chia Ch'ing Emperor to
confirm the accession to the throne of a new king of the Ryukyus
in 1800.

2 The Way of Living

This 'chapter' was presented in the World Book Company edition
as being Shen Fu's reflections on how one should get through the

---

* While we have confirmed the analysis of these appendices to our own satisfaction,
we are indebted for the original information to an article by Liu Fan in the 1 February
1937 edition of the *Kuo-wen Chou-pao*. His detailed and indignant article was titled
'The Forgery of the Missing Manuscripts of *Six Records of a Floating Life*'.

tragic business of life. In fact, judging from the title, that is probably just what Shen Fu intended it to be about, but it is not likely that we will ever know what his real thoughts were on the subject. For while this 'chapter' is more varied than the previous one, its variety consists only in that it lifts from more works.

The principal victim in this case is the *Summary of Maxims for Behaviour* written by a former Grand Secretary, Chang Ying (1638–1708). Chang's book was a collection of rules for personal conduct. He may have had personal experience of the need for such a book, as there are popular accounts that tell how the K'ang Hsi Emperor kidnapped one of his daughters-in-law and took her as a concubine.

Notes

1. 1763.

2. Originally designed in 1044, the pavilion – actually a large park – was restored in 1954. Shen Fu's home itself has recently been relocated by Soochow municipal officials and included in a list of historic buildings in the city that are considered 'worthy of preservation'.

3. This may be the first time some readers have encountered the Chinese practice of using multiple names; it will not be the last. In addition to a childhood name and a proper given name, all educated Chinese of the Imperial period had at least two others – a 'literary name' taken to express, usually, a desired attribute (Shu-chen means something like 'precious virtue') and a 'style', a sort of formal nickname. Both could be changed at will, making life interesting for later scholars.

4. *P'i-p'a Hsing*, a T'ang Dynasty poem by Pai Chü-i (772–864). It tells of the meeting between an official exiled to the distant South and a former courtesan from the capital who has been abandoned there by her merchant husband.

5. 1775.

6. 1780.

7. Such as would have been proclaimed on the anniversary of a previous emperor's death.

8. A famous Yüan Dynasty play by Wang Shih-fu and Kuan Han-ch'ing. The romance originated in the T'ang and has come down in several versions; this, the most famous, culminates with the dramatic capitulation of a young lady to the desires of a student. Its language is teasing and in places erotic, and Yün must have intended her casual reading of the book to be provocative.

9. Roughly, modern Shaohsing County in Chekiang Province.

10. An archaic name, even when Shen Fu was writing, for Hangchou.

11. From an ancient Chinese fable about a fisherman, that is here quoted from Mencius. Arthur Cooper explains the reference as meaning that while one cannot escape from the everyday world, one should still retain a portion of oneself unsullied by it (*Li Po and Tu Fu*, trans. Arthur Cooper, Penguin, 1974). A later version of the story from the *Odes of Chu* gave the Pavilion of the Waves its name.

12. Shen Fu is showing off his scholarship. His list roughly divides into

two parts, the classic writers and those who later defended the classic tradition against the incursions of more florid styles. We have here re-arranged the second half of Shen Fu's list – the names beginning with Chia- and Tung – to clarify the literary relationships among those mentioned:

The Annals of the Warring States is one of the earliest of the Chinese histories, covering the period 403–221 B.C. McNaughton believes the book was originally written as a handbook for orators and officials (William McNaughton, *Chinese Literature*, C. E. Tuttle, Tokyo, 1974).

Chuang Tsu was the name of a Taoist philosopher, supposed to have lived from 365 to 290 B.C., and gave his name to his canonical interpretation of the Taoist classic *Tao Te Ching*.

K'uang Heng was a distinguished prime minister to the ninth emperor of the Han Dynasty, who ruled from 48 to 32 B.C. He was said by his contemporaries to be the premier literary figure of his day.

Liu Hsiang (80–9 B.C.) was a prince and a minister of the Former Han Dynasty. He is remembered as a scholar, however, who revised *The Annals of the Warring States* and who wrote the unique *Biographies of Famous Women*.

Shih Chien was the literary name of Ssu-ma Ch'ien (145–?86 B.C.), the Grand Historian. His epic *Records of the Historian* chronicled the history of China from earliest times to his day.

Pan Ku (32–92 A.D.) wrote the *History of the Former Han Dynasty*, the first of the great Chinese dynastic histories.

Chia and Tung were Chia Yi (200–168 B.C.) and Tung Chung-shu (179–104 B.C.). They were officials of the Former Han Dynasty whose writings began to crystallize the 'classic' style of Chinese literature.

Yü and Hsü were Yü Hsin (513–581 A.D.) and Hsü Ling (507–583 A.D.). They lived during the Six Dynasties period (222–589), and were responsible for perfecting the more florid 'matched prose' style of writing which gradu-ally overtook the 'classic' style at that time.

Lu Chih (754–805) was a T'ang Dynasty prime minister, the style of whose memorials to the throne began a reaction against the overblown 'matched prose' style and a return to the more spare classic syntax which, in general, is the style of traditional writing that has come down to us today.

Ch'ang Li was the literary name of Han Yü (768–824), who took Lu Chih's lead and began the T'ang Dynasty's great literary revival of the classic style.

Liu Chou was a name taken by Liu Tsung-yüan (773–819). While he and Han Yü feuded about religious questions continually, they were the closest allies in the movement to restore the classical prose.

Lu Ling was the Sung scholar and official Ou-yang Hsiu (1007–1072). After its great revival in the early T'ang period, the movement for classical prose weakened and was overtaken once again by the 'matched prose' and several other styles. Early in the Sung period, however, Ou-yang Hsiu devoted most of his life to what turned out to be a lasting restoration of the traditional literary style.

Su Hsün and his sons were the 'Three Su's', Sung scholars who became Ou-yang Hsiu's allies in the movement to restore the classic style. After seeing his writings, Ou-yang brought Su (1009–1066) into the government, where his essays soon became a model for students. As Chief Imperial Examiner, Ou-yang awarded the highest degrees to Su's sons – Su Shih (1036–1101), better known as the poet Su Tung-p'o, and Su Ch'e (1039–1112). Between them, they carried the day for the classical style which dominated Chinese writing for the next 800 years.

13. Perhaps the greatest of the poets of the T'ang Dynasty, and among the greatest of all Chinese literature. Chinese who know no other poets know 'Li-Tu'. One wonders if Shen Fu was aware that neither of them ever passed examinations; Li scorned them and Tu failed them. Li Pai is usually known as Li Po, the poet whose stanzas gave this book its name and which begin our translation. While it is customary to give his name as Li Po, as it is pronounced in the Peking dialect, we have used Li Pai to provide linguistic continuity with the following lines.

14. Pai Chü-i. The T'ang poet was, of course, Yün's first teacher only in that his poem was the first thing she ever read.

15. 'White'; or 'pure'; also, a surname.

16. By saying she feared she would write many *pai* characters, Yün was making a dialect pun on their conversation to say she feared she would write many *pieh* characters; that is, characters written incorrectly.

17. A rhyme-prose form of irregular metre, archaic and most difficult.

18. The 'Songs of the South', from the fourth and third centuries B.C.

19. Notorious lovers of the Han Dynasty. Cho Wen-chün fell in love with Ssu-ma Hsiang-ju and ran off with him one night after he courted her by playing the lute at her father's home shortly after she had been widowed.

20. The Weaver's Star. The legend tells that the weaver and the cowherd were so much in love that they neglected both cloth and cows. Thus they were banished to separate stars, and can come together in the sky only once a year, on the 7th day of the seventh month of the lunar calendar. It is a day for lovers and for young women in search of a husband.

21. An extract of lime was a commonly used perfume in Imperial China.

22. In other words, Shen Fu, the man of gentle family in love with the impoverished Yün.

23. This is not adoption in the modern Western sense of the word. It implied a joining of two otherwise unrelated families, and a sponsorship of the child by his 'adoptive' parent. One could compare it with the Western practice of having godfathers and godmothers, though it had few religious connotations.

24. Thus giving the man a male heir to perform the proper funeral and memorial rites for him. Shen Fu would also have inherited property from his uncle, just as if he had been a natural son.

25. Readers who feel the discussion is becoming offensive are correct; it is the same in Chinese. The only explanation is that both Shen Fu and Yün were still quite young at this point, and that Chinese society is more comfortable with the subject of defecation than Western society; it enters into serious writings from Confucius to Mao.

26. A good woman remembered in many Chinese operas. Though ugly, she was made empress by King Hsün of the Northern Ch'i Dynasty (550–577 A.D.) because she reprimanded him for his poor government.

27. Imitation flowers made of small pearls, used as hair ornaments.

28. Yün dismisses her pearls with a reference to traditional cosmology. *Yin*, the female principle, and *yang*, the male, dominate all of nature and are ideally to be kept in balance, neither one overshadowing the other. Wearing pearls, Yün suggests, can lead to an over-concentration of *yin* in a woman; one of the many results of that is said to be a propensity to see ghosts.

29. The Five Sacred Mountains, focal points of Chinese cosmology for millennia, are scattered throughout the country. The other scenic spots Yün mentions would have been an easy trip from Soochow.

30. With which the couple is pulled together.

31. The character for 'fragrance' in the name Shen Fu gave their bedroom combines with the character for Yün's name to give the Chinese expression for rue, a fragrant herb.

32. Which, if it was square, would have made it about eighty feet on each side. (See Weights and Measures, p. 20.)

33. Chang was a boatman for the Yüan Dynasty salt monopoly who, somewhat to his surprise, found himself leading a rebellion in 1353 as the dynasty was collapsing. He quickly captured five prefectures near the mouth of the Yangtze River, and made his capital at Soochow. Chang declared his Imperial intentions in 1363 by proclaiming himself Prince of Wu, but he was captured and strangled four years later by the armies of Chu Yüan-chang, who went on to found the Ming Dynasty.

34. That is, Buddhist accounts of how actions in previous lives have their effect in this life.

35. Usually taken to be about a third of an English mile. (See Weights and Measures, p. 19.)

36. To the Dragon King of Tung-t'ing Lake, a popular deity in central China, generally in charge of watering the crops. Among his more spectacular accomplishments was said to have been the coercion of a mortal into marrying his daughter during the T'ang Dynasty.

37. Presumably to show that it was a woman's bound foot.

38. Being illiterate.

39. Readers who are suspicious about Shen Fu's relationship with the boat girl are probably on the right track.

40. 1794, in the traditional cycle of year names.

41. Modern Kwangtung Province.

42. A collection of temples and pagodas north-west of Soochow. It takes its name from a tiger that is said to have appeared there to guard the grave of an ancient king.

43. A euphemism for spending time with courtesans.

44. The *Lien Hsiang Pan*, a play by Li Yü (1611–?1680). Li-weng was his literary name. Yün's confirmation that she had this play in mind gives us our principal clue about just what her real relationship with Han-yüan may have been: the play tells the story of a young married woman who falls in love with a girl, and then obtains her as a concubine for her husband so the two women can be together. As van Gulik has pointed out, Imperial China regarded liaisons between women – as opposed to those between men – quite tolerantly. They did not by any means necessarily imply a lack of affection between such women and their husbands (R. H. van Gulik, *Sexual Life in Ancient China*, Humanities Press, 1974: he discusses female homosexuality on p. 163, and the play itself on p. 302, where he translates its title as *Loving the Fragrant Companion*).

PART II

1. Duck saliva being a supposed cure.

2. A county in north-east Anhwei Province, about 250 miles from Soochow.

3. Shen Fu is referring to what Li Chi, in *The Travel Diaries of Hsü Hsia-k'o*, calls 'scholarly graffiti'. Li quotes a Ming scholar as saying, 'It is disgusting to see inscribed stone tablets cluttering (the) foothills ... Even officials in this province get accustomed to this practice and make it a tradition, so that all the rocks are carved with inscriptions in red and white, making it a most distressing sight' (Li Chi, *The Travel Diaries of Hsü Hsia-k'o*, The Chinese University of Hong Kong, 1974).

4. A traditional Chinese building is not constructed of heavily walled rooms like traditional Western buildings. It consists, rather, of heavily timbered sections of framework joined one to another, from which lightly constructed walls are hung. It is these sections of framework that we have translated as 'spans', following Gernet and Wright (Jacques Gernet, *Daily Life in China on the Eve of the Mongol Invasion, 1250–1276*, trans. H. M. Wright, Stanford University Press, 1962). The exact size of a 'span' is indeterminate.

5. Traditionally, that part of Anhwei Province south of the Yangtze River.

6. A county in south Kiangsu Province famous for its pottery.

7. Ni Tsan (?1301–?1374), an eccentric painter from the Soochow area, regarded as one of the 'Four Masters of Late Yüan Painting'. He gave away most of his fortune, one of the largest of the day, and had great influence on Ming painting.

8. An island of the Immortals.

9. Buddha's Hands are the fruit of a mountainside tropical citrus plant; they are about the same size as, and closely resemble, two hands placed palm to palm in the fashion of Buddhist prayer. They are an aromatic, and are also used to flavour tea – in which case they are considered to be a cure for sore throats – and sweets. The modern version of Shen Fu's warning about the fruit's fragility is that it will spoil if touched by someone with oily hands.

10. An inedible medicinal citrus fruit of central China.

11. An archaic script dating from the Han Dynasty, which ended about 1,500 years before the *Records* were written. It is sometimes used in making personal seals.

12. A traditional woman's hairpins were long, made of precious materials, and valuable; selling them was a last resort.

13. A reference to deaths, certainly including Yün's.

14. Just under three quarts.

15. The following is a rough model of the Imperial examinations, except, of course, for the financial arrangements.

16. Who was thus unable to tell from the handwriting who had written which poems.

17. Two entries from each of six candidates ought to have yielded twelve couplets. Shen Fu had little taste for such details, however.

18. A 'cash' was a copper coin of Chinese currency. 'Incense money' is one of the polite Chinese expressions for a gratuity.

19. The Ch'ing Dynasty allowed close relatives of officials to turn in 'official' papers in the national examinations; they received preference.

20. Chinese rice wine is best drunk warmed.

PART III

1. 'Third lady' is a title of respect, and what Yün would normally have been called in the house. While 'third wife' is not impolite, it implied that the author had two wives senior to Yün; he did not, so use of this phrase was a snide insult to her.

2. North-east of Hangchou.

3. Yangchou.

4. Shen Fu's father is talking delicately about acquiring a concubine.

5. Modern Yicheng, in Kiangsu Province.

6. The author's younger brother, Chi-tang. It is a form of address that a wife is supposed to use in speaking of a brother-in-law who is not as old as her husband.

7. Yün had failed to refer to her husband's parents in the respectful terms proper for a wife to use.

8. It may not seem so, but this was a concession by Shen Fu's father; he was not insisting that the couple divorce.

9. Kwangtung and Kwangsi Provinces.

10. By a 'gold' Shen Fu presumably means a tael – a Chinese ounce – of gold.

11. A line from a famous poem that recounts the kidnapping of a beautiful woman by the barbarian leader Sha-shih-li during the T'ang Dynasty.

12. Thus saving her parents the humiliation of visiting the pawnshop themselves.

13. The Buddhist Hrdaya Sutra, also known as the Prahja Paramitra Sutra; it is central to the beliefs of Mahayana Buddhism.

14. The 'Westerner' is one of the greater puzzles Shen Fu gives us. The characters he uses are those normally used to describe a European, a non-Chinese, person; but a European money-lender in Soochow in 1800 stretches all probability. We can only guess, but perhaps the author was referring to a Tibetan, a Mongol, or a person of another of the West China minority races.

15. i.e. gentlefolk.

16. Shen Fu's father was giving him a choice of leaving home or of being prosecuted at law for filial impiety; it could be a most serious charge.

17. So that Yün's son-in-law would inherit the family's full estate.

18. A poetic reference to the fact that Shen Fu's father was Wang Chin-chen's uncle.

19. Thus Wang would bring her up and have the right to marry her to his son when she was older.

20. Between 3 a.m. and 5 a.m.

21. Just north-west of Soochow.

22. An ancient tale immortalized by the Chin poet T'ao Ch'ien (365–427), about a fisherman who strolls through a peach orchard and discovers a mysterious valley isolated from the cares of the world. On his arrival, he is interrogated by the inhabitants of the valley about conditions in the outside world, much as Yün was being questioned by the farm women. According to the legend, the fisherman began his trek by mooring his boat at Chuanchou on the Yüan River in Hunan Province.

23. Mrs Hua was excusing her neighbours' curiosity at seeing a city woman.

24. This sounds a strange procedure, but destitute Chinese gentlemen always seem to have been doing it. Presumably their undergarments were finely made of silk, and so were worth something. For another example, see Li Chi's *The Travel Diaries of Hsü Hsia-k'o*, p. 224. Shen Fu, by the way, needed the money to take a ferry across the Yangtze River, from Chiangyin to Chingchiang.

25. In south-central Kiangsu Province.

26. It was not unusual for a city to have two *yamen*, if it was the centre of two administrative units at the same time. Some old maps even show three

yamen in one city; see, for example, *The City in Late Imperial China*, pp. 354-5 (G. William Skinner, *The City in Late Imperial China*, Stanford University Press, 1977).

27. Foreign coins.

28. Yangchou.

29. The implication, confirmed below, is that he got his job as a favour from his friend.

30. A large one, that is, with a seat in which someone pushed him along. This was a not uncommon mode of transport, especially in the countryside.

31. The Yangtze.

32. By holding them responsible for the loss of their son.

33. A couplet from the T'ang poet Yüan Chen (779-831).

34. 1803.

35. This seems to have been a significant way for a candle flame to behave. A similar example, foretelling a good day to come, appears on p. 469 of David Hawkes's translation of *The Story of the Stone* (Cao Xuequin, *The Story of the Stone*, Volume 2: 'The Crab-Flower Club', trans. David Hawkes, Penguin, 1977).

36. The wooden tablet for a deceased person that is placed in the family's ancestral hall.

37. The original name for Yangchou. It means 'River Capital', and dates, as does the city, from the Sui Dynasty (589-618).

38. That is, settling his debts, a customary necessity at the end of each year.

39. Chih Sung-tzu is the name of an ancient Immortal. Shen Fu was saying he planned to leave home and become a recluse.

40. One of the heroes of the Three Kingdoms period (222-280 A.D.), later worshipped as a god.

41. Formal nickname.

42. The large island in the mouth of the Yangtze River.

43. Despite all his problems, Shen Fu is telling us, he still maintained the position of first precedence in the family.

44. Near the mouth of the Yangtze.

45. Which on the Chinese calendar marks the beginning of spring.

46. 1790.

47. The rebellion was a renewed outbreak by the secret society that had been plaguing Chinese emperors since the Yüan Dynasty.

Shih was a successful official, much of whose career is here recounted by Shen Fu. He was, however, dismissed from his post in Shantung in 1807 after a court case for which he was responsible was declared a mis-trial. This should have ended his career, but the Emperor, perhaps remembering important memorials he had helped draft during the fighting in Szechuan, gave Shih the rank of a compiler at the Hanlin Academy, the centre of government studies. Shih requested sick leave and escaped into retirement later in the year, however. He was only fifty-two at the time, and in the remaining thirty years of his life he became a noted scholar and calligrapher in Soochow.

48. This was presumably an adopted daughter of Shen Fu's mother. See note 23 to Part I, p. 151.

49. Huaiyang being still another name for Yangchou.

50. Shantung Province, called Shantso because on traditional Chinese maps it was to the left (*tso*) of the mountains (*shan*) of Taihang. It is in fact to the east of the Taihang Mountains, but traditional maps placed south at the top and, therefore, east at the left.

51. In other words, he had no money to keep in the sleeves of his robe. The implication is that he was an incorrupt, and thus a poor, official.

52. At first this may seem an irreverent and irrelevant act on the part of Shen Fu's old friend. But by giving him a concubine, which he certainly could not have afforded to buy himself, Cho-tang was trying to ensure Shen Fu had a son to survive him.

PART IV

1. South-east of Hangchou, in what is now Shaohsing County.

2. Firecrackers.

3. The Orchid Pavilion lies in the Shanyin area, and was made famous in a poem by Wang Hsi-chih of the Eastern Chin Dynasty (317–420). Yü's Tomb is also near Shanyin, and is supposedly the tomb of the king who is reputed to have founded China's first dynasty, the Hsia, in 2205 B.C.

4. Su Hsiao-hsiao was a famous courtesan of the Southern Ch'i Dynasty, which ruled much of what is now south China from 477 to 502 during the north–south interregnum between the Han and Sui Dynasties. Hsiao-hsiao seems to have been a woman of many delights, and a talented poet as well. She captured most of the hearts of her time, and her reputation fascinated poets long afterwards – among them Pai Chü-yi of the T'ang Dynasty and Su Tung-p'o of the Sung.

5. This was Ch'ien Lung's fifth tour 'south of the river'; he visited Hangchou and Haining, a county near by, in 1780, two years after Shen Fu's visit.

6. South of what is now Shanghai.

7. Just west of Soochow; it has a temple originally founded under the Liang Dynasty (502–557). Han Mountain – Han Shan in Chinese or, literally, Cold Mountain in English – is the name given to the authors of the sixth- to ninth-century poems who so influenced the poetry of the 'beat' generation in the United States in the 1950s.

8. The Chinese phrase for their dress could be translated 'we wore neither robes nor shoes'. In other words, they were not dressed as government officials.

9. Literally, 'wind and water', the Chinese concept of geomantic suitability, according to which sites are chosen for houses, graves, and other things.

10. Her name meant 'orchid', and this is a snide comment on her apparently Rubenesque figure.

11. Yang Kuei-fei was the courtesan who was rather plump and is supposed to have so distracted the T'ang Emperor Hsüan Tsung that he almost lost the dynasty to the rebel An Lu-shan. She was executed by loyalist troops at Mawei.

12. Yangchou.

13. The following is a description of the beauties of Yangchou, a city renowned for its scenery. It dates from about 590 as virtually a second capital, built by the second and last emperor of the Sui Dynasty. Yü-yang was the Ch'ing poet and official Wang Shih-chen (1634–1711). His most popular collection of poetry was printed in Yangchou about 1700.

14. 'Musical stones' have the most ancient of histories, and the most varied of meanings; the phrase can refer to ancient instruments that were part of the earliest Chinese musical theory, but here it refers to a stone gong used to call the monks to prayer.

15. Ou-yang Hsiu (1007–1072), a scholar of the Sung Dynasty ennobled for his work. A temple to him was erected behind the P'ingshan Hall after Shen Fu's time.

16. G. R. G. Worcester has described these boats, with a photograph, on pp. 208 and 209 of his *The Junks and Sampans of the Yangtze* (United States Naval Institute Press, 1971). He called them *k'uai pan ch'uan*, or 'quick plank boats'.

17. Just under seventeen acres. (See Weights and Measures, p. 20.)

18. Or more precisely, to the Ch'ient'ang River's junction with Hangchou Bay.

19. About twenty miles (See Weights and Measures, p. 19.)

20. The tides at the mouth of the Ch'ient'ang River that runs past Haining and Hangchou are among the world's more spectacular. The largest wave recorded there reached a height of over twenty-five feet and a speed of over thirty feet per second. According to legend, this tide once shifted an iron ox, weighing one and a half tons, that had been placed beside the river by an emperor to 'keep watch over the sea'. The tides are highest at the time of the Mid-Autumn Festival.

Another description of the tides has been provided by G. R. G. Worcester, who tells of the scene when quite large junks took advantage of the tidal current to get a free ride up the bay to Hangchou: 'The white, roaring wave breaks into a crest which grows higher as it advances through the ever-narrowing funnel of Hangchow Bay. Pandemonium breaks loose. The madly yelling junkmen fend off their boats from the stone wall and, smartly slipping their mooring lines, are afloat in an instant and are on their way to Hangchow in the wake of the bore. They usually do the twenty-three

miles in about two hours' (*The Junks and Sampans of the Yangtze*, p. 184).
A photograph of these ships is also included.

21. In south-east Anhui Province. Shen Fu may not have known it, but the youngest of the 'Three Su's' he mentions on p. 31 was magistrate of Chihsi for five years during the Sung Dynasty; it was a banishment.

22. Hangchou.

23. Over a hundred feet. (See Weights and Measures, p. 19.)

24. Yen Tzu-ling was banished from the court of his friend Han Wu Ti, so the tale goes, after falling asleep with his leg across the emperor's body. Edward Schafer explains how this fact combined with the appearance of a nova in the constellation 'Seat of the Divine King' to get Yen thrown out of the palace. He is said to have spent the rest of his life fishing from the terrace named for him on Prosperous Spring Mountain in Chekiang Province. For Schafer's account, see p. 268 of his *Pacing the Void: T'ang Approaches to the Stars* (University of California Press, 1978).

25. From the 'Second *Fu* on the Red Cliffs', by the Sung poet Su Tung-p'o (1036–1101). See p. 139 and note 87 to Part IV.

26. A leader of the Yellow Turban rebels at the end of the Han Dynasty.

27. Wang Meng (1301–1385), another of the 'Four Great Masters of Late Yüan Painting'. Closely associated with artists from Soochow, Wang took his courtesy name from Yellow Crane Hill near Hangchou, where he lived after he came to prominence.

28. Coins of copper, Chinese currency.

29. This also means coins of copper cash. As Mathews explains in his *Chinese–English Dictionary* (Harvard, 1975, p. 282), the reference is to an old legend that says if the blood of a mother water-beetle is smeared on eighty-one copper cash, and the bicod of her young on another eighty-one, the coins will always come together no matter how long they are circulated.

30. That is, inure himself to worldly desires.

31. The rebellion, in 1788, devastated much of north Taiwan and the shipping routes it dominated.

32. Kiangsu Province north of the Yangtze River.

33. Here, the reference is to Kwangtung Province and specifically to its capital, Canton.

34. The tenth month of the Chinese calendar, so called because it occasionally includes a warm spell.

35. In south-east Anhwei Province.

36. The reference is to Mencius, and this is one of his early rules of proper government. Dobson translates the entire passage: 'Do not disregard the farmer's seasons, and food will be more than enough. Forbid the use of fine-meshed nets, and fish and turtles will be more than enough. Take wood from the forests at prescribed times only and there will be material enough and to spare. With a sufficiency of grain, of fish, and of material, the people would live without anxiety. This is the first principle of Princely Government' (*Mencius*, trans. W. A. C. H. Dobson, Toronto Press, 1963, pp. 27–8).

37. Near Anching, in south Anhwei.

38. At Nanchang, Kiangsi Province. They were by now on tributaries of the Yangtze.

39. Modern Nankuan, in southern Kiangsi Province.

40. 'Long-life noodles' are a standard part of traditional Chinese birthday meals.

41. Chinese mountains seem to have been full of such admonitions. Again, Li Chi says that at a particularly frightening point on the climb up Hua Mountain in Shensi there used to be a stone inscription that said, 'Think of your parents' (*The Travel Diaries of Hsü Hsia-k'o*, p. 145).

42. General Mei was a talented warrior on the side of Liu Pang (247–195 B.C.), founder of the Han Dynasty.

43. General Mei's name means 'plum'.

44. The 'month of the winter sacrifice' is the last month of the year on the lunar calendar, usually falling in February on the solar calendar.

45. They had just crossed from Kiangsi into Kwangtung.

46. In north Kwangtung, on the southern side of the Tayü Mountains. From there they completed their journey by boat.

47. Just outside Canton.

48. The 'province city' being, of course, Canton.

49. A Cantonese expression for prostitute, with which, of course, Shen Fu was unfamiliar.

50. Shameen, in Cantonese. This island later became the centre of Western life in the city, after Canton was opened to trade under the treaty port system in 1843. Shen Fu was visiting it in 1793.

51. In the Cantonese which Shen Fu did not speak.

52. A euphemism for prostitute.

53. This may not be as sinister as it sounds. Small ornamental locks were sometimes worn as amulets, locking in the wearer's good fortune.

54. Through which the rest of the world was then allowed to trade with China, from August to March of each year.

55. The *Ch'ün Fang P'u*, a thirty-volume encyclopedia of Chinese plants by Wang Hsiang-chin, a scholar and official to the Ming Dynasty's Wan Li Emperor (reigned 1573–1620).

56. The author's literary name.

57. That is, out of the city walls and back to the flower boats.

58. Due west of what is now Shanghai.

59. Shen Fu has here adapted two lines from the poem 'Banishing Care' by the T'ang poet Tu Mu (803–852). The original poem reads:

> Wandering the country with my wine,
> I found the girls here so very fine.
> Ten years since I woke from Yangchou dreams
> With a bad name in pleasure houses.

60. 'Weito' is the Chinese name for a Bodhisattva, and the Weito Hall

of a temple is the room where two Bodhisattvas stand guard over the temple entrance.

61. Van Gulik attributes the melody to the flutist and scholar Huan I, who served the Chin Dynasty's Hsiao Wu Emperor (reigned 373–379) (R. H. van Gulik, *The Lore of the Chinese Lute*, C. E. Tuttle, Rutland, Vt., 1969).

62. An insult, to a monk. Yi-hsiang was presumably upset that the abrupt and unbecoming worldly curiosity of the monk should disturb their outing. It will be recalled that talking about official business was one of the activities forbidden by Shen Fu and his friends during their gatherings at the Villa of Serenity.

63. Fan Chung-yen, 989–1052. Born in a poor family during the Northern Sung Dynasty, he rose to be a great government official and scholar. He is remembered, among other things, for a saying expressing his view of the obligations of an official: 'First to worry about the problems of the world, last to enjoy the delights of the world.'

64. About ten feet. (See Weights and Measures, p. 19.)

65. Fourteen years before; see p. 106.

66. Wuling was the district from where the fisherman in T'ao Ch'ien's essay set out on the day he stumbled across the Peach Blossom Spring (see p. 81). Once he had left the Immortals' abode he was never able to find it again.

67. Twenty feet or so.

68. A picul, roughly 133 lbs. (See Weights and Measures, p. 20.)

69. Yangchou.

70. This is the old name for the city that became Shanghai. The old name meant 'On the Ocean'; the modern name means 'On the Sea'.

71. Yü Mountain is still a favourite tourist spot, north and east of Soochow.

72. A blend of tea.

73. An archaic measure equal to seven Chinese feet.

74. Ten feet. (See Weights and Measures, p. 19.)

75. He was probably going to use them as pigments for his paints, a common use for this kind of stone at the time.

76. From Shen Fu's description it is not possible to say exactly where this would be today, other than that it must be somewhere near the outer mouth of the Yangtze River, probably on one of the islands in the river mouth.

77. Tiger Hill is the collection of pavilions, pagodas, and temples just north-west of Soochow.

78. Traditionally, the site where the Wu king Ho Lü was buried with 3,000 swords in 496 B.C. Ho Lü is supposed to have sponsored the first use of iron in making swords, and to have founded the city of Soochow. His tomb is said to have given Tiger Hill its name, when a tiger appeared there to guard the Imperial resting place.

79. A garden originally laid out in 1350 as part of a temple.

80. Yün-lin was the Yüan painter Ni Tsan. See note 7 to Part II.

81. Built by King Fu Ch'a of the Wu Dynasty for his love the Lady Hsi-shih, whom Herbert Giles in his *Chinese Biographical Dictionary* (Chinese Materials, 1975) called one of the most famous of Chinese beauties. She was introduced to the king by an enemy who sought the king's downfall, and the strategem worked. Fu Ch'a was so infatuated with Hsi-shih that his rule soon collapsed, and he committed suicide in 473 B.C. Lingyen Mountain is south and east of Soochow.

82. Both of which are near Soochow.

83. South Anhwei Province.

84. Now part of the triple city of Wuhan, in Hupei Province.

85. Actually downstream from Wuchang.

86. A Han Dynasty book describing the rivers of China; the text as Shen Fu would have read it and as it exists now is thought actually to date from the Three Kingdoms period (222–280 A.D.).

87. They are two of the most famous poems in the Chinese language. Su (1036–1101) was a Sung Dynasty poet and, in writing about the battle of the Three Kingdoms period some 800 years before, he confused the cliffs at Huangchou (modern Huangkang) with the real site of the battle some eighty-five miles away. Having been made by a famous poet, it is a famous error. It is an easy mistake to make in Chinese, however, because the names of the two places sound so much alike – Shen Fu here comes close to confusing them himself – and it certainly did not hurt the poems.

88. Which would have made it about eighty feet on a side. (See Weights and Measures, p. 20.)

89. Chang (678–740) later became a minister to the T'ang Emperor Hsüan Tsung.

90. The famous philosopher and poet of the Southern Sung, who lived from 1130 to 1200.

91. Kuan Yü, a hero of the *Romance of the Three Kingdoms*, the novel of warfare and intrigue at the end of the Han Dynasty; the story begins in the year 220 A.D., with the famous phrase, 'Empires wax and wane; states cleave asunder and coalesce.'

92. Kuan Yü's famous mount.

93. Sung Yü was an official of the kingdom of Ch'u during the Warring States period which ended, for Ch'u, in 223 B.C. Yü Hsin served the Liang and Northern Wei Dynasties some seven hundred years later.

94. As they were away from family and friends, they had no one on whom to call.

95. A purple mist is one of the emanations that can be expected on the appearance of a remarkable person. Lao-tzu was the Taoist sage, and is supposed to have presented the original copy of one of that philosophy's classic, the *Tao Te Ching*, to the local governor at Hanku Pass.

96. Ch'ang Li was the courtesy name of Han Yü (768–824), one of the great literary figures of the T'ang Dynasty. Regardless of his feelings, one

should not be misled by Shen Fu's disparaging remarks about T'ungkuan. It controls the Yellow River crossing and a main road into Shensi, and was traditionally a position of great strategic importance. When Li Shih-min, founder of the T'ang Dynasty, was advancing on the Sui Dynasty capital at Ch'ang An in 617, one of the first things he did was to position a blocking force at T'ungkuan to prevent Sui reinforcements from reaching the city. Like most of Li's plans, it worked.

Seven hundred and fifty years later, a successful attack through T'ungkuan enabled the Ming Dynasty's founder, Chu Yüan-chang, to consolidate his hold on North China.

97. About half an acre. (See Weights and Measures, p. 20.)

98. Called *go* in Japan and by most Americans, the Chinese game is played with black and white stones on a board; each player attempts to surround the stones of the other.

99. The 'unmoored boat' has long been a symbol of melancholy, aimless life for the Chinese *literati*.

100. One of the mythical first emperors of China.

101. A *jen* equals seven feet. (See Weights and Measures, p. 19.)

Maps

A general map of East China, showing places to which Shen Fu describes travelling. The dotted line from Wuhu south is the route of his 1793 trip to Canton. On his trip west, note that he first went from Wuch'ang to Chingchou, then back to Wuch'ang; the track from Fanch'eng to T'ungkuan is only approximate.

Places Shen Fu travelled near his home of Soochow. The dotted line is the route of his trip from Hangchou to Chihsi. It should be recalled that at the time Shanghai barely existed; it grew to its present importance only as a creature of Western imperialist penetration of China in the mid nineteenth century.

1. City God Temple (Mountain)
2. South Screen Hill
3. T'ienchu
4. The Pavilion-in-the-Lake
5. The Jade Spring
6. The Agate Temple
7. Koling

8. Hsiling Bridge
9. Purple Cloud Cave
10. Ch'ient'ang Gate
11. The Chaoch'ing Temple
12. The Tuan Bridge
13. The Hsiaoyutien Gardens

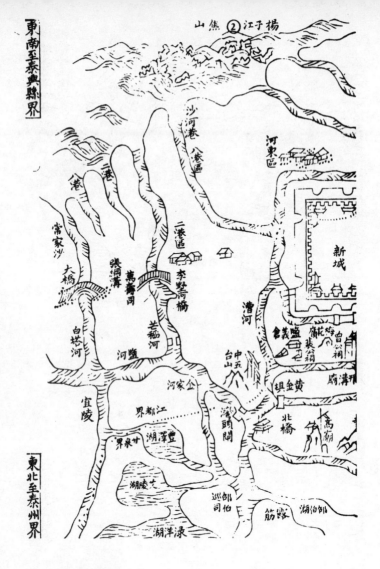

東南至泰興縣界

東北至泰州界

揚子江 ② 焦山

沙河巷 八巷遍

河東區

港 港

二港遍

常家沙 新城

大橋 張綱溝

漕河

嘉靖司 李墅橋

倉義鹽

白塔河 芒稻河 曾裴廟花

鹽河 廟溝祠

五中山台 白公祠

公家河 黃金壩

宜陵 江都界 橋北 高橋

甘泉界 潁頭閘 伯祠湖

豐澤湖

文陵湖 邗伯司 筋墓 湖伯邗

渌洋湖

1. Chin Mountain
2. Chiao Mountain
3. Rainbow Bridge
4. P'ingshan Hall
5. The Fifth Spring East of the Huai River

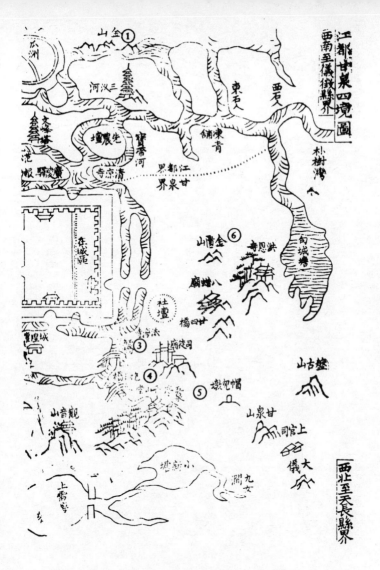

江都甘泉四境圖
西南至儀徵縣界

西北至天長縣界

6. Chinkuei Hill, where Yün was buried
7. The Hsiench'un Gate district of the city, where Shen Fu rented a 'house of two spans facing the river' when Yün moved to join him in 1802. It was in this house that Yün died

THE STORY OF PENGUIN CLASSICS

Before 1946 ...'Classics' are mainly the domain of academics and students, without readable editions for everyone else. This all changes when a little-known classicist, E. V. Rieu, presents Penguin founder Allen Lane with the translation of Homer's *Odyssey* that he has been working on and reading to his wife Nelly in his spare time.

1946 *The Odyssey* becomes the first Penguin Classic published, and promptly sells three million copies. Suddenly, classic books are no longer for the privileged few.

1950s Rieu, now series editor, turns to professional writers for the best modern, readable translations, including Dorothy L. Sayers's *Inferno* and Robert Graves's *The Twelve Caesars*, which revives the salacious original.

1960s The Classics are given the distinctive black jackets that have remained a constant throughout the series's various looks. Rieu retires in 1964, hailing the Penguin Classics list as 'the greatest educative force of the 20th century'.

1970s A new generation of translators arrives to swell the Penguin Classics ranks, and the list grows to encompass more philosophy, religion, science, history and politics.

1980s The Penguin American Library joins the Classics stable, with titles such as *The Last of the Mohicans* safeguarded. Penguin Classics now offers the most comprehensive library of world literature available.

1990s The launch of Penguin Audiobooks brings the classics to a listening audience for the first time, and in 1999 the launch of the Penguin Classics website takes them online to a larger global readership than ever before.

The 21st Century Penguin Classics are rejacketed for the first time in nearly twenty years. This world famous series now consists of more than 1300 titles, making the widest range of the best books ever written available to millions – and constantly redefining the meaning of what makes a 'classic'.

The Odyssey continues ...

The best books ever written

P E N G U I N (🐧) C L A S S I C S

SINCE 1946